Crafting Your
MESSAGE

Tips and Tricks for Educators to
Deliver Perfect Presentations

TAMMY HEFLEBOWER
with Jan K. Hoegh

Solution Tree | Press

a division of
Solution Tree

555 North Morton Street
Bloomington, IN 47404
800.733.6786 (toll free) / 812.336.7700
FAX: 812.336.7790

email: info@SolutionTree.com
SolutionTree.com

Visit **go.SolutionTree.com/leadership** to download the free reproducibles in this book.

Printed in the United States of America

Library of Congress Cataloging-in-Publication Data

Names: Heflebower, Tammy, author. | Hoegh, Jan K., other.
Title: Crafting your message : tips and tricks for educators to deliver
  perfect presentations / Tammy Heflebower with Jan K. Hoegh.
Description: Bloomington, IN : Solution Tree Press, [2020] | Includes
  bibliographical references and index.
Identifiers: LCCN 2019023398 (print) | LCCN 2019023399 (ebook) | ISBN
  9781949539493 (paperback) | ISBN 9781949539509 (ebook)
Subjects: LCSH: Teacher effectiveness. | Oral communication--Study and
  teaching.
Classification: LCC LB1025.3 .H44 2020 (print) | LCC LB1025.3 (ebook) |
  DDC 371.102/2--dc23
LC record available at https://lccn.loc.gov/2019023398
LC ebook record available at https://lccn.loc.gov/2019023399

Solution Tree
Jeffrey C. Jones, CEO
Edmund M. Ackerman, President

Solution Tree Press
President and Publisher: Douglas M. Rife
Associate Publisher: Sarah Payne-Mills
Art Director: Rian Anderson
Managing Production Editor: Kendra Slayton
Production Editor: Alissa Voss
Content Development Specialist: Amy Rubenstein
Proofreader: Elisabeth Abrams
Text and Cover Designer: Rian Anderson
Editorial Assistant: Sarah Ludwig

Acknowledgments

To Mike, my incredible life partner who is my biggest supporter and encourager. You helped me find my message. Logan and Nate—you *are* my messages to the world! Now, go fine-tune your own. Be bold. Be brave. Be the best version of you that you can be. Thanks for your love and guidance.

To my mom and my late dad. Thank you for helping me learn to use my voice to share hope, and to express my passion. You taught me the value of hard work, perseverance, devotion, and the gift of gab! Your sacrifices, support, and unending love pushed me beyond what I thought possible. I am forever grateful.

To my brother, Doug. Despite our age difference and dissimilar pathways, we've always found our commonalities. Your honesty, grit, and unending support modeled a friendship beyond family. As we've grown, it's been great to rekindle our sibling love and admiration. Thanks for who you are!

—Tammy Heflebower

Solution Tree Press would like to thank the following reviewers:

Michael Adamson
Director of Board Services
Indiana School Boards Association
Indianapolis, Indiana

Gayle Allen
Solution Tree Associate
San Francisco, California

Judy Curran Buck
Solution Tree Associate
Derry, New Hampshire

Pam Dean
Principal
Park Avenue Elementary School
Stuttgart, Arkansas

Jennifer Elemen
Educational Administrator
Monterey County Office of Education
Salinas, California

Anthony Grazzini
Director of PLCs and Special Projects
Cicero School District 99
Cicero, Illinois

Brad Randmark
Assistant Principal
Burnham School
Cicero, Illinois

Jon Yost
Solution Tree Associate
Clovis, California

Visit **go.SolutionTree.com/leadership** to download the free reproducibles in this book.

Table of Contents

Part 2
Processes and Protocols

Chapter 9
Team Building

About the Authors

Tammy Heflebower, EdD, is a highly sought-after school leader and consultant with vast experience in urban, rural, and suburban districts throughout the United States, Australia, Canada, Denmark, England, and the Netherlands. Dr. Heflebower has served as an award-winning classroom teacher, building leader, district leader, regional professional development director, and national and international trainer. She has also been an adjunct professor of curriculum, instruction, and assessment at several universities, and a prominent member and leader of numerous statewide and national educational organizations. Dr. Heflebower was the vice president and then senior scholar at Marzano Resources prior to becoming the CEO of her own company, !nspire Inc.: Education and Business Solutions. She also specializes in powerful presentation and facilitation techniques—writing and sharing them worldwide.

Dr. Heflebower is widely published. She is lead author of the award-winning book *A School Leader's Guide to Standards-Based Grading* and the award-finalist book *A Teacher's Guide to Standards-Based Learning.* She is coauthor of *Collaborative Teams That Transform Schools: The Next Step in PLCs* and *Teaching and Assessing 21st Century Skills.* She is a contributor to *A Handbook for High Reliability Schools: The Next Step in School Reform, Becoming a Reflective Teacher, Coaching Classroom Instruction, The Highly Engaged Classroom, The Principal as Assessment Leader, The Teacher as Assessment Leader,* and *Using Common Core Standards to Enhance Classroom Instruction and Assessment.* Her articles have been featured in *Kappan, Educational Leadership, Diversity Journal,* the *Education Week* blog, and the *Nebraska Council of School Administrators Today.*

Dr. Heflebower holds a bachelor of arts from Hastings College in Hastings, Nebraska, where she was honored as an Outstanding Young Alumna and her team was inducted into the hall of fame. She has a master of arts from the University of Nebraska Omaha. She also earned an educational administrative endorsement and a doctor of education in educational administration from the University of Nebraska–Lincoln.

Jan K. Hoegh has been an educator for thirty-plus years and an author and associate for Marzano Research since 2010. Prior to joining the Marzano team, she was a classroom teacher, building-level leader, professional development specialist, assistant high school principal, curriculum coordinator, and most recently assistant director of statewide assessment for the Nebraska Department of Education, where her primary focus was Nebraska State Accountability test development. Ms. Hoegh has served on a variety of statewide and national standards and assessment committees and has presented at numerous conferences around the world.

As an associate with Marzano Resources, Ms. Hoegh works with educators across the country and beyond as they strive to improve student achievement. Her passion for education, combined with extensive knowledge of curriculum, instruction, and assessment, provides credible support for teachers, leaders, schools, and districts. A primary training focus for Ms. Hoegh is high-quality classroom assessment and grading practices. She is a coauthor of the books *Collaborative Teams That Transform Schools* (2016) and *A School Leader's Guide to Standards-Based Grading* (2014), as well as other publications.

Ms. Hoegh holds a bachelor of arts in elementary education and a master of arts in educational administration, both from the University of Nebraska–Kearney. She also earned a specialization in assessment from the University of Nebraska–Lincoln.

To book Dr. Heflebower or Ms. Hoegh for professional development, contact pd@ SolutionTree.com.

Introduction

It was January. I had been in my role as an author and trainer at a renowned research company for three months, and I'd been asked to conduct my first keynote. The location—Montréal, Québec, where French is the primary language. I needed to learn not only about a new educational system but also about another country's existing approach to my controversial topic of effective grading practices. During my keynote, I stood behind a podium, stiff and stern. I had memorized my presentation. In my delivery, I used limited inflection, my pacing was too fast, and I had to pause for the information to be interpreted and understood. There was no physical space for interactivity, so I aborted such infused experiences. The topic, a philosophical shift for the audience, was another hurdle. When my address was over, the audience was polite, yet I knew it certainly had not been a home run. Rather, it was maybe a dive into first base after a struggle at bat. Afterward, I reflected. I learned. I revised. I committed to getting better, much better.

Selling your ideas is grueling! Whether you are presenting to a board, a team, or your staff, during a teleconference, or at an informal gathering, conveying and selling a poignant, memorable message takes specific knowledge and skills. Do you know these skills? Do you have them? Whether you are interested in capitalizing your skills as an educational speaker (an instructional coach, principal, professional developer, or superintendent) or whether you are a professional from another field seeking to learn and enhance presentation and facilitation skills, this book is for you!

This resource presents the culmination of my key learnings over the course of two decades of full-time public speaking, including training and speaking engagements, both nationally and internationally. I have presented to a myriad of audiences, which include local, state, and national boards; CEOs; service clubs; administrators; parents; business constituents; and trainers or facilitators.

This book is divided into two distinct parts: (1) tips for preparing for, delivering, and reflecting on your message, and (2) processes, protocols, and strategies to implement in your presentations.

Throughout the first part of this resource, each chapter focuses on a particular element of making a successful presentation and its many derivatives. Chapter 1 describes the important considerations and needs of adult learners. Thoughtful planning questions, as well as an organizational quadrant, help novice and expert presenters reflect about the meaningfulness and purpose of the message itself. Chapter 2 embodies essential elements of content, training formats, group-size characteristics, and considerations for planning short- and long-term work. The next few chapters highlight considerations for how to *deliver* a quality message. Chapter 3 describes important considerations for setting the stage—room arrangement, use of sound, managing the audience, centering yourself, and preparing the all-important speaker's toolkit. Whether you are a novice or an expert presenter, thoughtful planning solutions will help you improve your approach and messaging. Chapter 4 embodies essential elements for three types of introductions: (1) informal, (2) formal, and (3) topic-based. The plethora of considerations for a dynamic delivery of your message is the focus of chapter 5. It discusses attention-grabbers, voice control, presenter behaviors, engagement, visual enhancements, and webinars. Chapter 6 describes tips for designing visuals and print materials to use in your presentation, including slides, handouts, and concerns when presenting via a visual medium. Chapter 7 emphasizes the importance of obtaining and using feedback from your audiences. It establishes the importance of feedback by highlighting current research, and provides suggestions to assist with obtaining feedback that is specific, timely, and the appropriate amount. Chapter 7 also provides helpful reflective progressions that you may use for planning and reflecting on your presentations. Chapter 8 concludes part 1 by featuring various presenter tips, tricks, and troubleshooting strategies, such as how to cope with a difficult audience or audience member.

Part 2 takes a different tone as it presents new, useful strategies you can incorporate to optimize your presentation and fully engage adult audiences. Chapters 9 through 14 provide processes and strategies in the areas of team building, triggering thinking, processing and practicing content, consensus building, summarizing, and checking for understanding. The appendix contains useful technology links to enhance your presentations.

It is important to note that the essence of this educational resource is based on and quoted from the series of published works by Dr. Tammy Heflebower, found in *Presenting Perfected: Planning and Preparing Your Message* (2018); *Presenting Perfected: Dynamic Delivery* (2018); and *Presenting Perfected: Feedback, Tips, Tricks, and Troubleshooting* (2019). While those books focused on tips for all presenters, this book has been adjusted to focus on presentations by educators. Additionally, the processes, protocols, and strategies included in part 2 are entirely exclusive to this volume. I hope this culminated resource will assist you in becoming the best public speaker you can be. Go—be great!

PART 1

Preparing for, Delivering, and Reflecting on Your Message

Many educators, especially those in leadership roles, are required to speak publicly on a regular basis. This may be to small teams, during staff meetings, at board of education meetings, at parent nights, or at other similar functions. Yet, many of us received very little, if any, formal training on how to do so—at least, beyond that nerve-wracking required public speaking course in high school or college. This resource is your go-to guide! Within it, you will find practical supports for preparing a thoughtful message, delivering it in a polished manner, and assessing your performance and audience feedback.

There is no one specific way to use this resource. Jump around to specific parts of need, or follow it in chapter order; the choice is yours. If you are a seasoned presenter, you may start at the feedback and reflection chapter (chapter 7, page 59). Here you will discover ways to make a good presentation better. The small details make such a difference, and considering these reflective practices will make you that much better. You may also find part 2 (page 87) particularly helpful in honing a new process or protocol. If you are newer to regular public speaking, begin with preparing an effective message (chapter 1, page 5), and move through the chapters in a consecutive manner. You will find that each piece builds upon those before it, culminating in a well-crafted message with ideas for delivering it dynamically.

Chapter 1

Preparing an Effective Message

Proper preparation and practice prevent poor performance.

—Robert Pike

Adult learners are different, and teaching adult educators is vastly different from teaching students. At best, adult learners can be interested, inspired, and enthusiastic, and at worst, they can be irked, jaded, and disrespectful. Let's face it: some educator audiences will try to behave in ways they would never tolerate from their students. They may resist your greatest ideas and be wary of new, untested concepts. Often, this is because they have had experiences in the past that justified such skepticism. However, you have the power to prevent such negative reactions. How your audience responds is related directly to you and the message you are conveying.

This chapter takes an in-depth look into how you can tailor your presentations to be maximally effective in front of an adult audience. It begins by considering the needs of adult learners and introduces questions you can ask during the planning stage of your presentation to ensure you meet these needs. Advice for improving and augmenting your knowledge of the subject matter follows. Finally, this chapter discusses the differences that may exist in your audience members, specifically focusing on four distinct adult audiences, and provides useful ideas for how to present to an audience with diverse learning styles. All these features will help you better engage your audience and distinguish your presentation as different and inspiring.

The Needs of Adult Learners

In most instances, adults want to contribute and have their knowledge honored and respected. There are defining features of virtually all adult learning theories (Dunst & Trivette, 2012; Heflebower, 2018a; Knowles, Holton, & Swanson, 2012; Kolb, 1984; Schön, 1983, 1987). Summarizing what the various authors espouse leads to the following four key components of adult learning.

1. **Relevant:** Adult learners are task- or problem-centered rather than simply topic-centered. They need to know *why* your training is important to them: What problem might this solve? How might this make their lives easier? The useful past experiences and insights adult educators possess provide them with knowledge about what is likely to work and what is not. Although adult learners are more readily able to relate new facts to past teaching and learning experiences, clearly connecting relevancy helps them buy into your message (Rall, 2017). If it is not relevant to their needs, they are not interested.

2. **Practical:** Adult learners consider the immediate usefulness of any new information (Rall, 2017). They are more impatient in the pursuit of learning, and they tend to be intolerant unless they can apply useful connections between your message and their practical problems. Adults bring their own experiences and knowledge into the training; they appreciate having their talents and information recognized and used during a teaching situation. Simply put, adults like learning that provides them with practical activities that build on their prior skills and knowledge.

3. **Active:** Adults want experiential learning. Adult participants are mature people and prefer to be treated as such. They learn best in a self-governing, participatory, and collaborative environment. They need to be actively involved in determining how and what they learn; they need active rather than passive learning experiences (Rall, 2017). Adults are self-reliant learners, and prefer to work a bit more at their own pace.

4. **Positive:** Mature learners appreciate appropriate humor and elements of entertainment infused into the learning environment. Adults are more intrinsically motivated than most students; they are enthused by internal incentives and curiosity, rather than external rewards. Adult learners are sometimes fatigued when they attend trainings, so they appreciate any teaching approaches that add interest and a sense of liveliness. Use a variety of methods and audiovisual aids, and try to incorporate a change of pace—anything that makes the learning process easier.

Thinking of these key components while crafting your message will ensure you meet the needs of adult learners. Asking yourself the questions in figure 1.1 can assist in planning your message. These questions should guide your initial planning for each of the four key components of adult learning through an effective message.

Key Component of Adult Learning	Planning Questions for Consideration
Relevant	• How will your message meet the needs of the audience members? • Why would they want to know or learn it? • What's in it for them? • What problem will this solve? • How will this increase participant engagement or achievement? • How might your content and processes make participants' lives easier? • How will you define or suggest specific skills? • What defines proficiency? How will participants reflect on it?
Practical	• How will you recognize the existing experiences and needs of the group? • Will you provide print or online resources for review and use? • Will there be time for participants to apply or plan using the information shared during the session? • Will there be time for feedback to refine skills?
Active	• How will you use your training space for active involvement? • Will you be able to modify any activity for thirty to fifty more or fewer participants? • Will you need materials to increase participation (handouts, cards for sorting, sticky notes, markers, highlighters, and so on)? • Will you use specific groupings throughout the training? If so, what are they (for example, dyads, triads, small table groups, or around-the-room discussion partners)? • How will you model any teaching strategies you are proposing?
Positive	• How might you use appropriate humor to set a fun tone? • What might be a positive quote, picture, or video to instigate a mindset for learning? • How will you monitor your own verbal and nonverbal behaviors to ensure they are portrayed as positive in nature?

Figure 1.1: Planning questions for the four key components of adult learning.

*Visit **go.SolutionTree.com/leadership** for a free reproducible version of this figure.*

Using these components and considering the planning questions will assist you in creating a thoughtful message. A great application is to use figure 1.1 (page 7) immediately to plan something you are about to present to an educator audience. Color-code each component on four different-colored sticky notes. During your planning phase, draft responses to the questions on the corresponding colored sticky notes and place them on a large surface, then clump each sticky note around others of the same color. This visual approach helps you start to see how your message will flesh out during a training process as you consider the various needs of adult learners. The purpose is to achieve balance with your ideas. You want to be certain that you have some ideas representing each color of sticky note. This way, you will be thoughtful about your message's relevancy to your audience, practicality for immediate use, ability to actively engage others, and likelihood of infusing a positive tone. If you find you are missing a color, or you are too heavy in another, adjust accordingly.

Carl J. Dunst and Carol M. Trivette (2012) found that catering to different combinations of adult learning methods resulted in increased adult learner outcomes. First, they found that active learning was an important method of adult learning. They found that when adult learners are more actively involved in the learning process, larger effects about their knowledge, skills, attitudes, and self-efficacy are noted. Think about learning a new instructional strategy—maybe a new academic game to infuse into your training or classroom to increase engagement. When you learn the game by actually experiencing it, you get immediate feedback about what works and what doesn't. As opposed to simply passively reading about the game, this pattern of new information, practice, and feedback helps you learn the skill incrementally, and this experiential application of learning increases retention.

Time usage is also of the essence. Dunst and Trivette (2009) found that smaller amounts of chunked content increased adult retention, as did training settings that accumulated twenty or more total hours. Recall the academic game analogy. Each time you broke the new skill into its component parts (chunked), then practiced, your brain was creating neural networks for learning that part of the game. Doing these small chunks repeatedly, with settling time for the brain in between, increases the permanence of the skill. When planning the most effective use of training time, think *smaller increments* interspersed with *practice*. For instance, you may use a professional development day to introduce an idea and provide time for planning and implementation. Then you can discuss the application of an idea and refine it during regular meeting times, like professional learning communities. Using these smaller time frames to chunk, reiterate, apply, and modify during small-session follow-ups over a sample three- to six-month period of time increases learners' proficiency and application of the new concepts or skills.

In sum, adult learners approach learning in different ways than younger learners. They are more self-guided in their learning, they require learning to make sense, and they avoid learning activities that are simply about compliance. Because adult learners typically have more life experience than younger learners, when they are confronted with new knowledge or an experience, adult learners construe new meaning based on their life experiences and are more motivated to implement it into practice.

Content Knowledge for Adult Learners

As you plan your message, you will need to know and provide critical components of the information you are sharing. This often involves defining key terms and concepts as well as providing context or relevant background information. Read. Listen. Learn. Explore the topic in depth. You must be the person in the room who has studied the topic the most. It may not mean that you know everything there is to know, but it will be blatantly obvious to the members of your audience if you lack content expertise. They have come to hear you teach them. You'd best know it well.

You might decide to use the age-old six questions: (1) who, (2) what, (3) where, (4) when, (5) why, and (6) how—to begin or guide your content planning. Explain your motivation to engage in a specific topic. *Who* needs to know? *What* is the educational innovation? *Where* will this work? *When* might you use it? *Why* is this important? *How* might you do this? Answering these questions will help you think about the clarity and comprehensiveness of your message. It may also surface the cost–benefit analysis of resources like essential personnel, system readiness, and possible unknowns. Thinking through your message in this manner will also assist in anticipating possible questions from your audience.

Another way to exemplify your content knowledge is to know which experts and resources to credit and be ready to provide them as examples. It helps to not only know others in the field who write about the topic at hand but also offer tools to support the implementation of shared concepts or practices within your message. In other words, you have lived it, and you can provide examples of practice to your audience. Be certain to use virtual professional learning networks to augment your understanding as well. You may use a common Facebook group or Twitter chat by creating or using an existing hashtag that connects others with similar interests. For example, I am part of a presenters Facebook group. It is a closed group to those who are accepted, and the discussion is specific to presenter topics. Consider using direct quotes, pictures, or examples of successful implementation of your idea or topic in other schools or districts for additional relevance.

It is also important to ensure accuracy of the concepts you present. One way to do so is to support the current learning with research, when applicable. Use applied research and empirical evidence for substantiation. For example, you may use anecdotes or real-world observations that answered a question or helped obtain information. An example might be to share pictures or videos of teachers using or explaining the strategy you are teaching. Another way to augment accuracy is to provide real-life examples of research into action. When you can share examples of actual educators from various grade levels implementing your ideas, you strengthen your credibility. Consider personalizing the information to the location and the audience, strengthening concepts with personal or location-specific examples and stories.

Augment your substantial content knowledge with some form of quality message design. Heflebower (2018a) summarizes a training format that helps you think thoughtfully about your topic. This format recommends the following.

- Identify the purpose and outcomes of the presentation clearly and at early stages.

- Develop key ideas early.

- Use and organize appropriate materials to support your message.

- Use meaningful, purposeful, and engaging activities and interactive learning strategies.

- Check for audience understanding and input on a regular basis; provide a means for adults to ask questions in a public or private manner.

- Allow time for application and reflection.

- Provide adequate closure and effective summary.

Applying these suggestions helps you design a learning experience that has a natural flow, and accounts for how adult brains often absorb, sort, and apply information (Brookfield, 2006).

Four Distinct Adult Audiences

Audiences have some similar, basic needs. One is to be respected as adult learners. Adults come with knowledge and experiences that should be drawn on and cultivated. What will you do or say to honor that? Consider touching on what your audience brings to the table early on, during your introduction to the topic. Honoring your audience early pays dividends later. For example, asking groups to total the years of experience represented at their table, then totaling those for an entire amount of experiences represented in the room, is a wonderful way to encourage others to share and realize they have ideas to offer throughout the training.

Although audiences have comparable needs, they also have some distinct differences. Some presenters will consider using one of the many products or processes for ascertaining the differences about how adults learn and consider information. You may have heard of or experienced these yourself. These include, but are not limited to, True Colors (Adamo, 2014), CliftonStrengths (Rath, 2007), Emergenetics (Browning, 2006), and Compass Points (School Reform Initiative, n.d.a).

Although these types of categorizations all have unique characteristics and can jumpstart many great team-building activities, in this book I opt for a detailed construct more specific to *training* adult learners, modified from Weller and Hermann (1996, 2015). This classification serves as a great planning tool and gives insights that a presenter may often overlook.

Weller and Herrmann (1996), and Herrmann and Herrmann-Nehdi (1996, 2015) identify four types of unique audience members presenters should consider.

1. The first group is logical and methodical. These learners need the facts, the numbers, the research, the data. They require you to answer the question, Why?

2. The second important audience type includes creative and imaginative learners. They appreciate pictures, metaphors, and the big picture. They thrive on knowing how things connect and ways in which to visualize it.

3. The third type includes the more relational and emotional listeners. They appreciate your stories and having a chance to interact with others about the topic.

4. The fourth is the relevant and practical group. Most adults appreciate practicality and relevance, as I mentioned previously; however, some audience members thrive in this area of application, examples, and details.

As you read more about these four distinct audiences (presented in figure 1.2, page 12), consider which bulleted characteristics are most indicative of you, as an adult learner. Interestingly, that is the very type you will often plan for first and amplify naturally when conveying your message. You may notice you have some needs in all areas of the quadrant, yet one type is often most dominant. Pay close attention to the words and phrases that describe that audience type. Plan accordingly. Closely consider the category diagonally from your strength area, as it consists of characteristics more opposite of you. It is the one you are most likely to overlook or even forgo when you are pressed for time. Consequently, paying particular attention to your message so that you address each quadrant helps enhance your message for all types of audience members. It is helpful to ensure that each portion of the quadrant is acknowledged for each major point or chunk of content. In fact, using the planning quadrant depicted in figure 1.2 will augment your preparation (and, later, your delivery) of an effective message.

These variations in audience member characteristics and corresponding suggested phrases will help you in planning an all-inclusive message.

Not only are there various types of learners within an adult audience, but there is also a suggested process—an audience planning cycle—for addressing each of the various learner types throughout a presentation.

1. First, begin with the facts and figures; meet the needs of the logical thinkers. Capturing them early on will help them listen (and even tolerate) later messages and experiences. Once the members of this group know what you are discussing works, they will listen. Yet, do not overdo this, or you will alienate the other audience types. One or two key facts, figures, or charts will likely suffice.

Logical and Methodical		Creative and Imaginative	
• Mathematical • Statistical • Example-focused • Problem solver	• Technical • Factual • Performance-based • Achievement-oriented	• Visual • Pictorial • Metaphorical • Possibilities-oriented	• Curious and playful • Risk taker • Entrepreneurial • Big-picture-focused
Phrases to connect to this group:		**Phrases to connect to this group:**	
"The facts are . . ." "Research from ___ concludes . . ." "According to experts . . ."		"Imagine this . . ." "Consider these options . . ." "What if . . .?"	
Relevant and Practical		**Relational and Emotional**	
• Relatable • Example-focused • Sequential and detail-oriented • Realistic	• Doer • Information user • Reliable and predictable • Cautious	• Storyteller • Musical • Trainer or facilitator • Expressive • Reflective	• People person • Compassionate and sensitive • Talker • Connector
Phrases to connect to this group:		**Phrases to connect to this group:**	
"Here's how this could work . . ." "You could use this to . . ." "A simple solution might be . . ."		"Have you ever felt like . . .?" "Others might feel . . ." "Once this happened to me . . ."	

Figure 1.2: Four distinct types of audience members.
Source: Adapted from Weller & Hermann, 1996, 2015.

2. Next, consider the relational and emotional participants. Create your message with the people involved. Who will be affected? Where can you accentuate compassion through a story or a quote? Connect the *people* to the topic.

3. After that, consider moving toward the creative thinkers. Here is a great place to share a metaphor to model possibilities. Use some creativity by involving the group in a visual depiction.

4. Then, follow with practical examples of others who have tried or experienced the topic firsthand to reach your relevant and practical members.

It is important to note that this is not the *only* way to approach the group through the lens of audience types. You may find a particular group is primarily composed of only a couple of the quadrant areas. For instance, imagine that you are asked to speak to a group of mathematics teachers. By nature of the discipline they teach, they are more logical and mathematical. This does not mean you should exclude the other areas of the quadrant but rather know thy audience. If you are working with a group of visual and performing arts teachers, you will likely encounter those with more of the visual and creative strengths. If you are uncertain, ask. You might provide a four-question Google survey, containing one question from each area of the quadrant, for the audience to complete prior to your training, to help you understand their strengths and needs. By all means, appeal to the masses first. Yet, if you are new to this idea, using the planning cycle in figure 1.3 may prove beneficial.

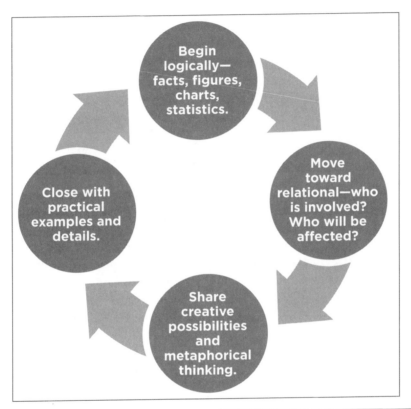

Figure 1.3: Audience planning cycle.

As an example of how to use the audience planning cycle, consider the design for a new mini-presentation, titled *From Perspiration to Inspiration: A Flash on Fitness*, to be given in a forty-five-minute breakout session at a district conference. The presentation will involve quick reminders and strategies within the following four areas: (1) physical, (2) mental, (3) sleep, and (4) nutrition.

The presenter begins by selecting one of the four topics listed—in this case, choosing to begin with *physical*. He or she then uses the sticky note strategy (see page 8), placing information from each quadrant of adult learners onto a separate sticky note. For example, when considering *logical* informational items, the presenter adds two notes. The first one reads, "The CDC cited 80 percent of Americans don't get the recommended 2.5 hours of moderate exercise per week." The second adds, "Adults should also engage in strengthening exercises twice per week." These two examples present facts and figures to appeal to the logical learners.

Next, the presenter lists ideas for the *relational* area. One sticky note reads, "Have you ever tracked your physical fitness in one week?" Others ask, "How many of you have some sort of fitness tracking device on your watch or phone?" and "Everyone go to the week of February 3–10, and look at your schedule. Is there any time to include 2.5 hours of physical activity that week?" Another sticky note indicates that these questions are planned to lead into a physical activity. The idea is to turn on some upbeat music and provide participants with the options of engaging in some physical activity right in the room. The options include marching, walking, jumping jacks, or scissor kicks for one full minute. Afterward, the presenter will ask participants to record their heart rates.

The *creative* section is the next area of focus. The presenter posts a few sticky notes in this section. One reads, "What if you scheduled your physical fitness like you do a required meeting?" Another idea is, "What if you connected your physical activity to another routine event, like taking a shower or eating breakfast? You don't complete one without the other." The presenter plans to provide a story for emphasis and humor at this point—an idea that is listed on another note.

The presenter then considers the *practical* examples. He or she notes, on a sticky note, a connecting phrase to reach out to this group: "Here's how this might work . . ." He or she demonstrates by displaying a picture of a calendar in which "physical activity" is listed. Another sticky note displays the idea of using a device-based activity tracker and noting the weekly summary. Considering an activity for the audience, the presenter notes an opportunity for tablemates to converse about how they find time to infuse physical activity. He or she plans to listen in to the discussions and have a couple of participants share their responses. The presenter notes another idea to teach (or reteach) the group the Fox method for monitoring individual heart rates for maximum benefits (Waehner, 2019). This method helps women and men calculate their maximum heart rate (220 minus age for women; 220.5 minus age for men), as well as their target ideal heart rate (80 percent of the maximum).

Although more details, visuals, and stories will likely be included in the presentation, the presenter has now fleshed out one major portion of his or her presentation in a way that will appeal to each audience member, no matter the learning style.

As a final consideration when planning your message, please don't poach. When you state another's idea, give them credit. When you share a quote or an excerpt, ensure it's carefully cited. Be mindful of taking the intellectual property of a great introduction, a funny story, or a catchy phrase. Always, always give credit to others when due. And try to use your own stories and examples—they will be better received because they are authentic.

Summary

This chapter highlighted the important considerations and needs of adult learners. It detailed some thoughtful planning questions as well as a useful organizational quadrant to help presenters reflect on their meaningfulness and purpose when crafting the message itself. Chapter 2 will help you take your message into the delivery phase.

Chapter 2

Planning the Delivery

> *Because ultimately presentations are about the*
> *audience, not the speaker.*
>
> —Akash Karia

This chapter will address essential elements of group size characteristics, roles, and considerations for planning short- and long-term work through various formats. These ideas will help you plan for the *delivery* of a quality message.

Planning for Audience Size

Audience size is an important consideration. In fact, the size of the audience will invariably dictate the type of energy in the room, the types of activities possible for interaction, and the way in which a presenter will pace the content and delivery. For example, seasoned speakers often concur that a group of fewer than twenty is one of the most difficult with which to work. The overall energy in this group size is far less than that of larger groups. One negative attitude is more pronounced and permeated. Everyone has to participate, and it is more difficult to get the sound of mass voices into the room. As one of my colleagues once said, "In a small group, everyone has to get the intended humor. Yet in a larger audience, just over half can respond to the humor, and it will feel as if the entire group does" (K. Williams, personal communication, April 29, 2015).

Comparatively, with larger groups (more than fifty-one), there is often a natural energy—almost a buzz. Although it takes longer to conduct active participation, the sound resembles a competition for airtime. Think of when you go dining at a restaurant or shopping at a retail store. Listen carefully—there is music playing. For the masses, silence feels awkward and unnerving. In fact, there is a certain type of music, tempo, and volume level known to create an actual state of attention in the brain (Feinstein, 2006). A discussion of appropriate music use occurs in chapter 3 (page 27), but the point is, sound matters. Music and voices create energy in the room. You want, and need, them both—but how to best utilize them will depend on the size of your audience.

Use figure 2.1 to consider the similarities and differences among various audience sizes. In so doing, think about your group size preference. Does your topic work best when presented to a specific size of audience? If your topic lends itself better to a smaller audience, then suggest that (or even require it) in planning. Often, you may not have control over the audience size. In that case, reference the chart to help you tailor your topic and activities to the size of your audience. For instance, you simply cannot get large groups of over two hundred people up and moving a great deal without thoughtful planning and space. Rather, using a standing meeting conversation with those nearby may be a better option to increase engagement and encourage discussion but not create chaos in the room.

Audience Size	Energy	Activities	Pacing
Fewer than 20			
20–50			
51–100			
101–200			
Over 200			

Figure 2.1: Audience size planner.
*Visit **go.SolutionTree.com/leadership** for a free reproducible version of this figure.*

Figure 2.2 is a completed audience size planner to reference for comparison. This figure details the features seasoned presenters might suggest.

Audience Size	Energy	Activities	Pacing
Fewer than 20	• Energy is limited. Infuse more instructional processes that involve exploration of the topic followed by group discussions, increased active processing options, and fewer direct instruction practices. • Fewer participants can dramatically decrease the energy you feel in the room. You may find yourself actually working harder to solicit engagement and responses. Therefore, consider options for a discussion format. Rearrange the room to accommodate a U-shape or circular formation using fewer, if any, tables. Aim to make the room cozy and comfortable.	• Dyads and triads work best for occasional discussions. • Use more whole-group discussions that feel conversational instead of like a presentation. • Participants can see and use charts effectively.	• Monitor for changing up activities every twenty or so minutes. Small groups may be able to go a bit longer if you use group conversation protocols. • Microphones are optional, and may even feel awkward in this size of group.
20–50	• There is more energy than in smaller groups, yet it is a bit more limited overall.	• Continue with smaller group sizes (two to four) for discussions. You have more options to vary the discussions. Use some paired discussions and some table team discussion formats. • It is easier for participants to network throughout the sessions. Encourage them to do so. • Stirring the group and colleague cafés work well with this size of group. • Use large-group activities with all participants occasionally, yet less often than with your smallest group size. • Charts still may work, but need large print size to be seen by all.	• Monitor for changing up activities every twenty or so minutes. • Microphones are encouraged. Even when people say they can hear, they can't hear easily. When in doubt, use a microphone and pace accordingly.

Figure 2.2: Completed audience size planner.

continued ↓

Audience Size	Energy	Activities	Pacing
51–100	• There is solid and more consistent energy in the room than in smaller groups.	• Continue with smaller group sizes (two to six), but vary it with some paired discussions and some table team discussion formats. • Movement is possible in most sizes of rooms, so build in such processes. • Large-group activities done with a model group of participants often work best. Rather than having everyone do an activity, have a select group of ten model it. • Teams of four work well. • Charts will be too small for this size of group. You will need to project your ideas and information onto large screens. • One large screen or multiple screens may be necessary.	• Monitor for changing up activities every twenty or so minutes. • Microphones are required. • Pacing will slow a bit with microphone use.
101–200	• Great energy. Laughter permeates the room.	• Movement is still possible as long as the room is capable of having some large spaces for such activities. • Large multiple (two or more) screens will be necessary.	• Monitor for changing up activities every twenty or so minutes. • Microphones are required. • Pacing will slow a bit more with microphone use and room size.
Over 200	• Great energy. Laughter permeates the room.	• Audience movement is limited. Standing at or near seats may work. • Small dyads work for brief conversations. • Large multiple (three or more) screens may be necessary.	• Monitor for changing up activities every twenty-five to thirty or so minutes. • Microphones are required. • Pacing will slow extensively with microphone use as the room echoes.

Using this chart as you plan your presentation helps you acknowledge how group size dynamics play into the way you structure your delivery and processing activities. If you anticipate a very small group, you will want to add in more print or web resources to allow for the small group to explore the topic in depth, whereas with a larger audience you may use more direct instruction and fewer, if any, large group discussions.

Considering Your Presentation Role

Presentations occur in various formats. Sometimes an educational host (principal, district leader, or educational service unit provider) requests a short presentation to inspire and overview a topic—a *keynote*. Other times, more in-depth *training* is needed. Yet other times, *facilitating* a group toward a consensus is warranted. There may even be times to do small-group or personalized *coaching*. Whatever the role of the presenter, it is imperative to understand the differences between these presentation roles as well as your presenter tendencies. Here, I describe the variations among these roles and responsibilities.

Keynote Speakers

Keynotes are sessions that last typically from forty-five to ninety minutes. They are focused on a single topic and are primarily intended to overview the topic and entertain the audience. Keynotes are often delivered in large ballrooms where it is difficult to get much participant involvement. Thus, keynote speakers need to be engaging in their presence and with their content. A solid keynote speaker most often addresses one or two key ideas, builds an overview of the content, and amuses the audience a bit along the way. Keynote speakers rarely "get into the weeds" by practicing the topic information or providing time for application of the ideas; that is not their purpose. Rather, a keynote address is more of an executive summary regarding a focused subject.

Not everyone can keynote, nor does everyone want to. In many cases, excellent trainers and facilitators cannot effectively move into the keynoter position. Likewise, some keynoters are lousy trainers or facilitators. Diane DiResta (2018) suggests "the best speakers stay in their lane." This means that presenters should be aware of who they are and capitalize on their strengths of being either more of an entertainer or a content speaker. DiResta (2018) recommends that entertainers opt for the modes of keynoter or emcee, whereas content experts may prefer the role of trainer.

Although certain types of presentations may feel more natural to certain presenters, it *is* possible to exchange lanes. Entertaining qualities will enhance trainings, and a topic focus will augment a keynote. However, the presenter must be very experienced and skilled. He or she must also know the strengths and limitations about each type of presentation, as well as how to adjust content and processes to fit the new lane appropriately. However, this takes considerable time, reflection, observation, and practice.

Trainers

Training sessions may range from a few hours to full or multiple days with the same audience. The goal of a training is for participants to acquire new information, techniques, or skills, or to transfer learning at a later time (Wild, 1999). Examples might include training about an instructional framework, standards-based grading practices, or behavior management techniques. Great trainers have specific content and processes to teach, and they must be able to communicate the message effectively as well as understand the audience's specific needs. Trainers are versatile and must command an audience for longer periods of time than keynote speakers. They use a combination of direct instruction, practicing activities, practical examples, video components, and group discussions to maintain their audience's attention for long periods of time. They must build relationships with audience members in order to obtain and maintain the respect and attentiveness of audience members. Often, trainers possess a deep content knowledge and have many practical experiences and examples to share. They really help audiences understand the topic in depth, and move them into application of key concepts. Trainers are also more in command of the time spent on each component, the types of activities used, the resources necessary, and how the learners will master or obtain the skills being taught. This is where the planning quadrant plays an important role. Thoughtfully applying the quadrant to each major training point ensures variation with intentionality.

Facilitators

Facilitators help groups accomplish a common goal or set of goals that they often could not accomplish alone. Unlike trainers, facilitators require less in-depth knowledge about a topic, but must have masterful people skills. A skilled facilitator helps groups accomplish common goals with synergy and success, helping others face difficult, sometimes less obvious issues with creativity and collaboration. Examples might include school board work sessions or leadership retreats, school- or district-led trainer or facilitator subcommittees, administrative team discussions, K–12 principal events, or even some professional learning communities. The end result is to achieve unanimous, win-win types of solutions. Facilitating an audience may last a few hours to one full day at the shortest, and multiple days or a series of intermittent days to accomplish longer-term goals.

Trainers are less concerned with collective thinking and common, collaboratively generated endpoints, and more about teaching specific content and processes to be used afterward. Trainers know the end result. Facilitators often do not. Instead, they help the group work cohesively toward an end goal. As Hunter (2007) said, "Facilitators are called upon to fill an impartial role in helping groups to become more effective. We act as process guides to create a balance between participation and results" (p. 150).

Facilitators must master the art of questioning—knowing what types of questions to ask and ways to elicit open-ended responses that enable stronger collective dialogue, perspective analysis, and inclusiveness of the group. Although the end result is to achieve unanimous, win-win types of solutions, it is truly the journey that is skillfully facilitated. They lead with phrases like, "Tell me about your thinking," "Please give a rationale for that perspective," "Who agrees with that train of thought?" and "I can hear that you are concerned about . . ." These strategies foster genuine interest in the viewpoints of each group member. It is important that each member feel heard, all the while realizing that the group-think is ultimately more important than the self-think. The journey is truly as important as the result.

Creating and adhering to norms are critical parts of the facilitation process. Consider starting with a short list of suggested ideas and then soliciting input from the group. As you do, define behaviors and hold people accountable to abiding by them. Write these norms down. Be sure your agreed-on norms are visible for all to see, and easy for you and others to reference during a meeting.

If you are relatively new to the facilitation process, start small. Consider mediating groups in limited scope and size, like family meetings, church groups, book clubs, or even friend misunderstandings. The more you practice strategies and questioning tactics, the more competent and confident you become. Gather a variety of group processes to expand conversations and work toward agreement. A variety of such protocols can be found in chapter 12 (page 137), including *dot voting, ranking,* and *idea survivor.*

Coaches

A coaching role is personalized, confidential, and somewhat complicated. A great coach recognizes the uniqueness of individuals and situations. Coaching conversations vary in pacing and styles (Wild, 1999). Similar to facilitation, coaching involves asking thoughtful questions and providing examples and direction as needed. A coaching situation is most often one-on-one or with a very small, trusting group of adults. The primary goal is to develop skills and to reflect on and improve individual performance. Sometimes, coaching involves instructional coaches leading coaching conversations with small teams or individuals. It might also include principals leading instructional coaching conversations as part of, or outside of, the formal evaluation process.

All roles are important to the teaching and learning process. None is necessarily better. Yet the objectives and considerations of each are unique. Figure 2.3 (page 22) presents a useful process for helping to identify the nature and characteristics of various delivery modes. Using this figure, consider the various roles and what makes each role exclusive in the training and content delivery. Work through figure 2.3 on your own or with your training partners. Draw on your experiences to discern the differences among the various roles and considerations. Then, compare your thinking to the completed example in figure 2.4 (page 23).

Role	Description	Objectives	Unique Considerations
Keynote speaker			
Trainer			
Facilitator			
Coach			

Figure 2.3: Presenter roles and characteristics.

*Visit **go.SolutionTree.com/leadership** for a free reproducible version of this figure.*

By better understanding the various presenter roles, you can recognize what type of presentation is warranted and what skill sets will be necessary to meet the outcomes requested of you. Expanding your knowledge may also help you as you grow your repertoire of presenter skills, stretching you to experiment with the variations by crossing into different roles and providing additional services or supports to groups.

Using a Process Observer

To enhance your practices in each of these roles, consider having a process observer. This may be a trusted friend or colleague. Have him or her watch you as you facilitate a group, and provide procedural feedback. Some questions for consideration might include:

- Was I able to treat all participants fairly and equally?

- Did I acknowledge all contributions similarly?

- Was I able to stay on topic?

Role	Description	Objectives	Unique Considerations
Keynote speaker	• Short time frames (forty-five to ninety minutes) • Requires clarity in message	• Keynoter-directed • Limited content • Elements of entertainment • Limited practice or discussion	• Short handout with key points • Slowed pacing • Carefully monitored stage movement
Trainer	• Breakout session, full-day to multiple days • More direct instruction interspersed with activities and applications	• Specific content and objectives provided by host • Learning blended with practice • Monitoring audience to direct pacing, responding to questions, and adding clarification	• Controls pacing • Preplanned and created activities necessary • Handouts helpful
Facilitator	• Varied time frames; full to multiple days • Often used during retreats • Consensus and collaboration imperative	• Goal for all to participate • Focused area of emphasis • Considers pathways and processes to accomplish outcomes • Group often identifies the outcomes together	• Not in control of exact outcomes or endpoints. Rather, these often emerge from the group processes and discussions led by the facilitator. • Requires flexibility and on-the-fly thinking • Skills needed in listening, redirecting, and tactfully handling unique adult behaviors • Handouts less necessary—often more charting or action-planning templates involved
Coach	• Short time frames (thirty to forty-five minutes)	• Coachee-focused • Supportive • Offers ideas as needed	• Questioning skills required • Listening and redirecting skills imperative

Figure 2.4: Completed presenter roles and characteristics.

- Did I catch the group members when they went off topic and realign them?

- Was I able to avoid alignment to one side or position? Did my comments give any member of the group the impression that I have a closer relationship or more agreement with him or her than the other group members?

- Was I able to involve participants by focusing on engaging participation, rather than evaluating the quality of the ideas being generated?

- Was I able to stand strong, even in the face of conflict within the group?

- Was I able to maintain neutrality and avoid judging any person or idea in conflict?

Quality feedback on these questions will help you improve your delivery and presentation immeasurably.

Addressing Time Frame Constraints on Content

Skilled presenters know their content well enough to consider variations in what can be accomplished in certain time frames. Typical options range from ninety minutes to multiple days—a considerable range to which the presenter must adjust. Variations in presentation time will invariably affect the depth of the audience's content understanding and the ease of implementation of ideas. This section will assist you in planning content for both short- and longer-term presentations.

Considerations for Shorter Presentations

What is your primary message? What is the soul of your information or idea? It is imperative for you to identify your core message, because that is what you share in your shortest time frame. Becky Blanton (2009) underscores the importance of selecting a core message, stating, "Convey one strong idea. Take time to focus each idea you want to express, then pick the most compelling, the strongest idea." That pared-down primary message should fit neatly into a ninety-minute overview. Think of it as applying a keynote perspective to your core message. Done well, this type of communication may actually be your "interview" with the audience members. In other words, this is a chance for others to see what you present and how you present it within that abbreviated time frame. If they like it, they will sign on for more. One method for showcasing this type of presentation might be at a local or statewide educational conference.

Considerations for Longer-Term Presentations

Some schools, districts, or other educational agencies may want (and even require) multiyear projects. When audience members sign on for more, they are embarking on a longer-term learning opportunity. These may range from a few days to a few years. Some topics (like implementing standards-referenced grading) are long-term endeavors that need thoughtful pacing and implementation over time. Such longer-term work requires you to think about the primary, secondary, and tertiary content and process chunks important to your overall topic. Simply put, *chunking* is the breakdown of your content into significant portions. What chunks come first, second, and so on? As you plan out multiday presenting opportunities, consider how you will organize your information into various time frames. These might include multiple overviews with subgroups. Then, move into deeper training sessions with cohorts (those learning together for a period of time), interspersed with activities and application.

Remember to consider the various perspectives of your audience members. Will you deliver a portion of your message to the leadership team? Although similar to the message you give to the whole staff, your leadership message will have nuances about leading the work. Those actually doing the work must deeply understand your messaging for use over time. Take advantage of the longer-term presenting format to build in follow-up and implementation supports for this group to enhance the learning and application of your message. These may occur face-to-face, via webinar, or even through a phone consultation. As you plan, ensure you consider a brief review of key content prior to adding new information. This will help solidify previous learning and provide the brain with the connected neural networks to which the new content must attach.

To solidify your understanding of the considerations necessary to present to both short- and longer-term audiences, consider how you might present a ninety-minute version, a half-day version, a full-day version, and a two- to three-week version of your content. When you have your ideas for these typical formats solidified, you can easily modify them to fit other, unique presentation time frames. Use figure 2.5 to outline your message points for the variations in time.

Time Frame	Key Message Points
Ninety-minute overview	One key point, or simply an overview of the topic
Half day (four hours)	One or two main chunks of content, expanded upon with practicing activities
Full day (seven hours)	Four or so major topic chunks presented with practicing activities and time for application
Multiday (twenty or more hours)	All content pieces addressed thoughtfully and thoroughly, with practice, application, and feedback elements infused

Figure 2.5: Message points for different presentation time frames.
*Visit **go.SolutionTree.com/leadership** for a free reproducible version of this figure.*

Planning for New and Existing Staff

Remember to consider the needs of various experience levels when designing your presentation plans. Honoring those who may already have some experience, or different experiences from those who may be brand new to the company or entity, is critical. This exemplifies that you know the differences between audience members. It demonstrates that you respect those who bring knowledge and experience into the presentation setting. The following are a few questions you might consider as you make your short- and longer-term plans.

- Who is new within the past year? How might these individuals' needs differ from the needs of veteran staff regarding your message?

- What do all groups need to hear and learn?

- How might you vary activities for the differences in experiences?

- How will you find out who is in the room? Will you do that ahead of time or during the introduction to the day?

Plan carefully for the diverse audience members within your training. Be certain to address those needs throughout both short- and long-term proposals.

Summary

Throughout this section, I highlighted essential planning elements regarding group size characteristics, presentation roles and formats, and considerations for planning short- and long-term work, as well as the need to think about various audience member experiences. Preparing your content and processes thoughtfully is an important first step in successfully fine-tuning your message. The following chapter delves into the importance of setting the stage for your message delivery.

Chapter 3

Setting the Stage

I try to create an environment where, when we step onto the set, we're all in character.

—Vin Diesel

Prepare your setting for success by ensuring your training or speaking room and arrangement complement your message. Think of this preparation work like prepping a painting surface prior to painting a room, setting a table for a big meal, or sowing soil for planting—excellent preparation prevents pitfalls. In this section, I highlight topics for consideration to include the room arrangement, use of sound, audience management, and your own self-grounding and preparation.

Arranging the Room

The arrangement of your room is paramount. Be certain you have spoken about this during your planning call or meeting with your hiring agency. You want to be certain that the room is arranged to maximize the training experience. There are dozens of arrangement suggestions. In the following sections, I detail a few common types with their corresponding characteristics and rationale.

The U-Shape

The U-shape (see figure 3.1, page 28) is great for groups of ten to twenty people. It allows for everyone to easily see and hear one another. This format works well for small-group trainings or facilitated sessions, team meetings, retreats, and board meetings. It allows for a presenter or facilitator to be positioned at the open portion of the U, and for participants to be comfortably seated around the outside of the rest of the tables. The U-format allows for much interspersed dialogue. One cautionary note, however, when using this format is to ensure participants have plenty of personal space in between one another and are not seated near the table legs.

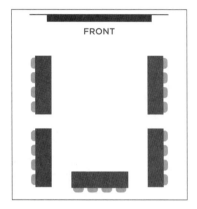

Figure 3.1: The U-shape room arrangement.

The Arrow

This arrangement is likely the most common, and is my personal preference. It can be used with both large (a few hundred) and small groups (twenty to fifty). In this formation, the presenter is placed at the front and center of the room, with rectangular tables angled at an arrow pointing toward the front and center. Tables positioned closer to the front will need a stronger angle, and those in the middle of the room will be perpendicular to the presenter. In this arrangement, all participants can see quite well, and no one is seated with his or her back toward the presenter. Ensure the tables are wide enough to allow participants to spread out and converse. Thin tables may need to be doubled in order for the personal space to be adequate. See figure 3.2.

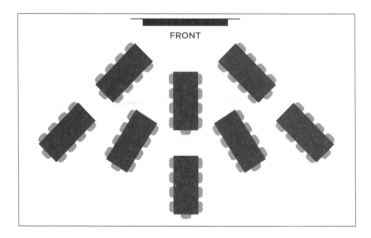

Figure 3.2: The Arrow room arrangement.

The Rounds

Using round tables with seats around them works for groups of up to one hundred or two hundred, and it easily enables conversations among participants. This format allows for grouping people more easily, and visually implies collaboration. If possible, only seat participants in a C-formation around the back side of the round table. This way, there is an open space at the front of the round where no chairs are located, which prevents having participants with their backs toward the presenter or blocking the view of people at the back of the table. If you must have chairs all around the table, physically turn the chairs toward the table so they are now facing the presenter. See figure 3.3.

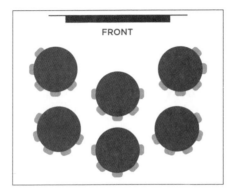

Figure 3.3: The Rounds room arrangement.

The Auditorium

Auditorium seating (see figure 3.4) works for hundreds to thousands of attendees. The format consists of fixed seats in rows with small or no table attachments. Sometimes there is a balcony, oftentimes not. The purpose is solely for participants to listen—signifying a "sit and get" perspective. In fact, in auditorium seating, it is difficult, but not impossible, to interact effectively. Use paired discussions or standing paired discussions to add some interaction. One advantage to this setting is that acoustics and technology tend to be high quality. However, this format is my least favorite for any training lasting longer than an hour.

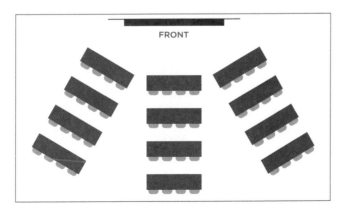

Figure 3.4: The Auditorium room arrangement.

The Conference Breakout

This seating often consists of slim tables in long rows with chairs facing forward. Typically, this setup is used for fifty to one hundred people in a tight space, such as hotel breakout rooms. It is sometimes called *classroom* style. It allows for limited participation and most focus to be toward the presenter at the front of the room. See figure 3.5.

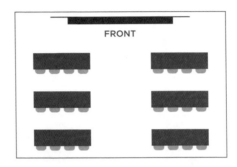

Figure 3.5: The Conference Breakout room arrangement.

Whatever the initial setup of your room, be certain it fits your presentation needs. In other words, if you need to angle the tables or move chairs so no backs will be toward you, by all means, do it. The arrangement will immediately suggest and even dictate your interaction capabilities. If you don't like the arrangement, get there early and move it to best meet your needs. I can't emphasize this enough—if participants cannot easily group, they won't do it. You will lose the effect of your presentation if the arrangement of your room impedes your work.

When planning room arrangements, also attend to the following.

- Use comfortable chairs with padding and fabric covers. Have just enough, if not even fewer, chairs set out than you might need. You want a room to feel full; empty chairs create black holes of energy deprivation. Instead, have additional chairs and tables on hand to easily add for overflow. It's better to add than to subtract.

- Allow for appropriate spacing among adults—minimally twelve inches between seats, allowing eighteen to twenty-four inches for each person seated. Adults need space for personal items and movement. Please note that this is not typically how room arrangers place chairs, so you will need to specifically request this amount of personal space for your participants ahead of time.

- Ensure that the room arrangement coincides with the type of training, activities, and physical movement you have planned. If you expect the entire group to move, is there a large enough space designated for that? However, be flexible. You may have to modify your delivery to manage a difficult room setup. No matter how much you plan, you will sometimes have to adjust on the fly.

- Use tables if participants will need to use additional materials (handouts, sticky notes, and highlighters). Ask for such items to be in containers on the tables.

- No matter the table type, arrange the tables with pathways and walkways so you and your audience members can easily maneuver the room. Walk in and among the chairs as you are testing your audio equipment to ensure you have the space you will need to move effectively.

Monitoring Sound

The sound in the room is important. If participants enter a silent room, it feels empty and stark. You want the room to look and sound inviting.

Using Music

When selecting music, consider what research has taught us about our brains. Music is one of the best condition changers. As Rich Allen (2008) reminds us, "At the very least, music can enhance motivation, attentions, and feelings of vigor" (p. 113). When you want an audience to be calm and relaxed, play music that matches the average resting heart rate of 60–80 beats per minute (bpm). Or, if you want the audience to be energetic and upbeat, play music that is twice that tempo—roughly 120 to 130 bpm. One way to determine the tempo is to find the beat of the music and count it for six seconds, then multiply that by 10 (to total 60 seconds) in order to find out how many beats the song selection plays in one minute. Then, create various playlists to match the states you want your audiences to emulate. I have playlists for opening music, closing music, reflection, lunch, and breaks. Use music for transitions, or even consider using a specific callback song cuing participants to return from an activity or break (Allen, 2008). Be mindful of variations in music appreciation. I tend to use well-known types of popular songs right before I formally begin. For instance, I have used "I'm So Excited" by the Pointer Sisters just prior to conducting my training, and "Who Let the Dogs Out?" by Baha Men to close a training. This one adds some humor, and the lyrical puns are intentional.

When playing music, the volume should be at a level that is noticeable, but not too loud. You should be able to greet participants without shouting. Also, be certain you abide by copyright laws and obtain your music appropriately. Apple Music or Spotify are great resources to purchase your music and easily organize your songs for use.

Using Microphones

When in doubt, use a microphone. Figure 2.2 (page 17) emphasized the importance of using a microphone, and when it makes most sense to do so. Here, I detail the effective use of the microphone.

Address microphone needs prior to your delivery. Do you prefer a handheld, lapel, or over-the-ear microphone? If you aren't sure, test out the options. If you do not use many visuals and consequently need a handheld clicker, a handheld microphone might work well. Many lapel microphones allow for your hands to be free. This is key if you use a lot of gestures and movement. Yet, lapel microphones can easily lose the sound with a presenter whose head moves often. Additionally, lapel microphones work best when attached to a tie or lapel collar. This does not always work as well with women's clothing and with the higher timbre of women's voices. If you are female, you must also be mindful that what you wear can impact your successful use of the type of microphone you will have at the site. A dress without a belt can be disastrous, because you may have no obvious place to clip the microphone pack. Having to hide a microphone pack can be uncomfortable and unsightly, and holding a microphone pack in one hand while speaking looks unprofessional. To avoid this, you may consider an over-the-ear microphone connecting system. These produce high-quality sound, and they come with an assortment of attachments that fit various microphone packs. I would highly recommend investing in your own microphone. I prefer a Samson, over-the-ear microphone. Using your own system will not only make you feel more comfortable, but also portray professionalism. Most independent microphones come with at least four of the most common adapters to be used with the typical microphone packs schools and districts have on hand. You will be accustomed to how the microphone feels on your ear, and the sound quality you will get is often superior to those you obtain at most educational sites.

Test the microphone early, before too many participants (if any) are in the room. Be mindful that, as the room fills with people, the sound will be absorbed, which can change the volume needs considerably. Keep technicians available for slight tweaks just before and after you begin. Ensure you have the sound loud enough to easily project your voice at various emphasis levels. Say phrases you will use in your presentation, and annunciate normally. Ensure the sound is rich, not tinny or echoing. Often, you will need to adjust the gain levels on the microphone pack in order to enhance the quality of the sound.

Master microphone control. That means be certain you remember to turn your microphone *on* when speaking to the group, but *off* when you are not. You don't want your microphone on when your audience is engaged in table conversations or when individuals are asking you a question not intended for the entire room. We are all aware of authentic presenter experiences when the microphone was left on as the presenter cleared his or her throat, coughed, or, yes, used the restroom. Always remember to manage that microphone!

Novice presenters often forget to turn buttons on and off, as they are nervous and preoccupied with all the many other details of the presentation. Practice shutting the mic on and off a number of times. Get a feel for the lag time it takes for the sound of your voice to amplify into the room, as well as how the button feels. If you place the microphone pack in your pocket or on the back of your body where you cannot see it, determine and remember the on and off button positions. Each pack varies noticeably. Some are push on and off, some have a switch, and still others require you to hold a button down for a period of time. Be sure you know which method works for your pack.

I recommend not allowing a technician to turn your microphone on and off for you throughout the presentation. Although it is a thoughtful gesture, technicians may get distracted, forget, or simply not be aware of your on and off preferences. As rudimentary as this seems, managing your microphone and the sound of your voice is the sign of an experienced speaker.

Managing Your Audience

Help your audience be respectful of your time throughout your presentation. When you take breaks, it is important to get your audience members back in their seats and attentive when you need them. Your actions help the participants manage their responses.

Embedding Timers and Countdowns

Consider using timers and countdowns. These help your audience better mind the time frames for breaks and lunch, and most assuredly get you started on time. Few things are more distracting than when the emcee or presenter is haphazardly trying to get the group's attention to start. You can find oodles of electronic timers online. Simply search for *animated timers*. Some will have sound, but you can simply mute the sound or add your own music to it if the default sound is not to your preference. I also like embedding countdowns into my presentation, so as to keep me from toggling back and forth between or among software programs as the presentation is underway.

Beginning on Time and Ending Early

It is imperative that you start your presentation on time. You immediately send a message about your expectations and those you will use with your group when you honor the time of those who are prompt. If, for some unforeseen reason, you must start a bit late, be certain you announce it. Begin by verbally honoring those who were there on time by sharing your appreciation, and indicate that you will begin in five minutes.

As important as beginning on time is, ending a bit early is also essential. Yes, you heard that right—early. Five minutes early is completely acceptable and allows for your host to wrap up with necessary announcements. Never, ever go over your allotted time. Never. It's a sign of disrespect and lack of planning.

Preparing a Filler (Just in Case!)

Create a set of filler options you can use as needed in case you run low on time. This might include a few additional slides, a story, or an activity that could be used to close a gap of remaining or dead time. Think of this as similar to a riff that musicians use when doing improvisation. They are given free rein to expend time creating and grooving a solo. A filler is a presenter riff. Use fillers as needed to uplift energy, provide active participation, or change the audience state. Often in all-day training situations, there are five to ten minutes before a scheduled break or lunch, where a planned riff is warranted. I often have a related set of slides and an activity that allows for me to extend to fifteen to twenty minutes, if needed. Many times, you will not need these options. However, it is sensible to prepare them just in case, and to know which topic-related riffs you will embed.

Centering Yourself

You are about to do something most fear—present to adults. Don't take that lightly. It's difficult. In fact, it's downright frightening for most, and debilitating for many. Find a way to center yourself prior to entering the presentation location. It might be a few minutes in your car, backstage, or even in the restroom. Wherever you can take a few deep breaths, capture a calming moment, or give yourself a bit of positive self-talk, find the time and do it. That moment of calm will help you deal with the frazzle or frenzy you may encounter as you arrive. There will be people to meet, hands to shake, a setup to complete, and unanticipated problems to solve on the spot. Be certain you've lowered your anxiety with a calming practice before you enter your location.

Remember to hydrate before, during, and after your presentation. Water should be your drink of choice while presenting. Although you may crave other drinks, those can come later; caffeinated drinks paired with unexpected nerves may make you jittery and tense. Carbonated beverages paired with a microphone can be embarrassing (think inadvertent belching or hiccupping). Water—good, old-fashioned water—is best. Some presenters refrain from taking in fluids, as they worry about needing to use the restroom too often. Actually, your body will crave the hydration and adjust (in most instances). Bring your own water, and plenty of it, in the container you favor. Never rely on someone else to provide something as essential to your presentation as water. Having your own plentiful supply will help you perform optimally.

Preparing a Speaker's Toolkit

Seasoned speakers have often learned the hard way that it is important to have a *speaker's toolkit* of resources and paraphernalia they might need onsite. The checklist in figure 3.6 might be a useful starting point as you create your own toolkit.

Consider anything you will need to effectively facilitate an activity you are using. Never assume you will have technology support to assist you, so learn about connectors, power sources, and sound boards. Be prepared. Additionally, always pack your own resources, and refrain from informal discussions upon ending your presentation until your supplies are packed. The reason for this is simple: everything has a place, and if you get distracted by talking, you will likely leave something behind. You will be stymied and stressed if you leave an important item, like your computer, a microphone adapter, or your clicker, at a previous venue.

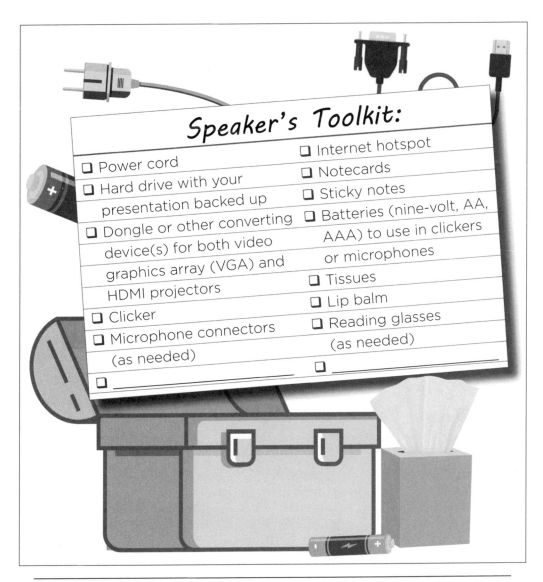

Figure 3.6: Speaker's toolkit checklist.
*Visit **go.SolutionTree.com/leadership** for a free reproducible version of this figure.*

Summary

Throughout this chapter, I highlighted the significance of setting the stage for a great presentation—from room arrangement and use of sound, to managing both your audience and yourself. The next part of this resource details the components of effective introductions and conclusions.

Chapter 4

Creating Effective Introductions and Conclusions

*We don't know where our first impressions come
from or precisely what they mean, so we don't
always appreciate their fragility.*

—Malcolm Gladwell

Introducing yourself and introducing your topic are both challenging, yet these are two of the most important things we do when presenting. Closing effectively is equally as demanding. In this chapter, we first explore your informal and formal personal introductions. Later, we discuss ways to introduce your topic and culminate your closing.

An Effective Introduction

A great introduction is well planned, and it gives you a chance to (Karia, 2012):

- Build connections with your audience
- Create a first impression that will determine your audience's receptiveness toward you and your message
- Set the tone for your time together
- Grab audience members' attention within the first thirty seconds so they don't mentally check out

- Put yourself a bit at ease to relax and obtain confidence with the group

A realization in quality presenting is that it is one thing to be a recognized communicator and presenter with your local work team, and another to be strong in a company. Likewise, it is hard to be a strong presenter at the regional or statewide level, and even harder to do so at the national and international levels. The reason is simple—*relationships*. When you have relationships with your audience members, they cut you some slack, and they are more understanding because they know you. However, in many presenting gigs—at least the first time—you are presenting to an unknown audience in an unknown place. Although your audience may feel they know you through a prior reputation, you begin your relationship building through an effective introduction.

Informal Introductions: What to Do

Whether you like it or not, you are *on* from the minute audience members first see you until you are far gone from the parking lot. Therefore, a few tricks of the trade will help.

Arrive first. You must be there before your audience arrives to ensure everything is ready—to make sure the room arrangement, technology setup, sound, print resources, and temperature are all perfect. As audience members arrive, you are in informal greeting mode. This requires you to personally greet as many participants as you can. The following considerations will make you more successful when thinking about your informal introduction techniques.

1. **Smile:** This seems trite, yet remember, you will be thinking about a dozen other things, and those concerns and stresses will likely show on your face. Practice your smile. Yep. Practice it. It should be genuine.

2. **Touch, if possible:** In some way, offer appropriate touch as you informally introduce yourself to your participants. There is truly something magical about it. The handshake is still the most common form of touch. Be sure your handshake is strong and single-handed, but not overpowering. Ladies, you *must* have a strong handshake. No mush hand, no pinch-like handshake. Look each person in the eye and shake his or her hand for about two seconds (longer gets competitive, shorter is awkward) while welcoming and introducing yourself. Of course, be mindful of cultural norms regarding handshakes or touch to avoid offending anyone.

3. **Share a verbal welcome and an informal introduction to each person you possibly can:** I elect to use my first name only, as both my names together are a mouthful. I also think it sends a more informal and conversational style. You may even find yourself going from table to table to do these informal introductions.

Say something as basic as "Welcome. Thanks for coming" or "Hello. Glad you are here!" Ask (and remember) people's names. Say people's names back to them. Use a few of the group members' names in your first half-hour of time together.

These incidental and informal introductions immediately connect your audience members to you. They send a clear message that you are personable and relatable, and that you sincerely care about participants taking the time to be with you.

Formal Introductions: What to Do

There are a variety of effective ways to craft a formal introduction of yourself to the group. The following are a few suggestions for consideration (DiResta, 2018; Karia, 2012; Pike, 1994). Select one or a couple you can merge together, which you will master and repeat easily.

1. **Begin with a unique story:** Stories are personal and connect your audience to you immediately. They can help you create a mind metaphor and will help your audience see you in a more human light. Ensure your story is, in fact, yours. What story is signature to you? Do you play an unusual instrument? Are you a baseball or soccer mom? Do you live in a unique area of the country? What makes you different from others presenting on the topic or during the conference? When you think about those differences, you will forge your signature story. Then, enhance it. Make it come to life through the senses. What did something smell like? How did something feel? Try to infuse some emotion (hopefully, joyous emotion) into the room.

2. **Craft a catchy phrase, or "a phrase that pays":** This memorable phrase may serve as an anchor for the rest of your presentation, upon which you will build your key points. Consider some catchy phrases you know and recognize: "Just do it!" "Every kiss begins with Kay." "You can do it; we can help." These offer a creative way to capture attention and introduce your topic.

3. **Use a thoughtful set of questions to get your audience thinking and wondering:** For example, you may ask, "Who is your favorite leader? What makes him or her great?" This question immediately focuses your audience on something of relevance you will later connect to the topic. It also frames the topic in a positive way.

4. **Help the audience identify a problem:** What is a problem the audience is likely experiencing at that moment? Name it. Begin by stating it. Put words in people's mouths: "I'm sure you were

hoping for a blizzard," "I bet you have more stress than most other occupations," or "Selling a product is so difficult these days." By identifying a problem, quickly followed by the promise of a solution or ideas to help, you will pique the interest of your participants.

5. **Share a powerful quote as another effective way to begin or enhance your introduction:** A quote can say just the right thing, without you actually having to say it. It helps you identify a feeling, a need, or a concern within the audience, while deflecting the genesis away from you. In other words, it can put a topic into the room without it being personalized to you. For example, Thomas Edison's famous quote, "Genius is 1 percent inspiration and 99 percent perspiration," may be a great way to open a discussion about effort and hard work. You might consider a different quote for a topic on planning an important message, like Effie Jones's famous quote, "Failing to plan is a plan to fail." The quotes focus your message and are exemplified by others' words. Consider them as a connector for your audience.

6. **Utilize an interesting fact or figure as yet another way to grab your audience's attention:** "What is the number-one concern for leaders?" "Why do most people hate their jobs?" "Why are we such an advanced country, yet still have such issues with poverty and homelessness?" These are examples of questions that connect you to your topic, and make the audience begin actively thinking.

7. **Reference something notable that just happened prior to you speaking (Karia, 2012):** Did you notice the exorbitant number of roundabouts on the way to the training? Did something silly occur in your hotel (that is appropriate to share)? Did the downpour everyone just experienced cause a particularly interesting situation for you? That reference can become a brief, yet appropriate and personalized story.

8. **Begin with something really unique about where you are speaking or the topic at hand:** Is your location the smallest in the area, so there is no stoplight? Does the location have a unique fact about which most, if not all, would relate to? Is there a favorite sports team competing in a big game? Learn about the area, as doing so always helps audiences appreciate the effort you took to know more about them.

It is not enough to consider the approach to your formal introduction. You must carefully plan it, practice it, and deliver it. Do so, repeatedly. You want your words to flow, your timing to be perfect, and your formal introduction to really grab the attention of your audience. Your introduction sets the tone for the rest of your time with the group. Make it strong. Make it great!

Begin planning your introduction carefully by selecting one of the previously mentioned ideas as an attention grabber, or by creating one yourself. Write it out. Yes. Stop right now, and write it out. You can begin with key concepts, maybe even jotted on sticky notes. Eventually, build your introduction into sentences and paragraphs. This is important!

Next, read every word aloud, carefully. Read it again. Do you have the perfect phrasing? Do you catch yourself stumbling over a few words? If need be, change them. If you stumble now, it is likely you will do so later in front of your audience. A great rule of thumb is to have a maximum of ten to twelve words in any one sentence (P. Gordon, personal communication, November 1, 2011). The rationale is simple: your audience listens in chunks. If your phrases are too long, your audience gets lost in wordiness. Go back to your introduction and count the words you have per sentence. Be sure that your sentences vary in length, and that there are thoughtful transitions between any key points.

Formal Introductions: What Not to Do

Introductions can, and often do, fall flat. That first experience with your audience may exhibit some negative audience behaviors, like sighs, eye rolling, and unsettled physical movement. As a presenter, this may quickly make you feel self-conscious and concerned about their receptiveness. To avoid this reaction, guard against the following characteristics of *ineffective* introductions.

1. **A *me-focused* introduction (Karia, 2012):** No one wants to hear your entire biography—no one! When speakers make the first few minutes (or more) all about forcing the audience to listen to them and their plethora of accomplishments, it feels self-centered and stuffy. You do not want your first few minutes to leave an audience wondering who the training is really for and about. Is it simply a chance for you to hear yourself talk about you? Or, is it going to be about connecting with your audience in an authentic way to foster listening ears and an open mind? Audiences can readily identify insincerity. If you display this, you will have lost them before you actually begin.

2. **An opening with the obligatory gratitude:** We have all heard presenters open with the following phrases: "Thank you, (host). My name is _____. I am so happy to be with you. I'd like to introduce myself." As Akash Karia (2012) says, "Unfortunately, most presentations today have very boring, predictable openings that turn audience members off" (pp. 21–22). This introduction feels obligatory to your audience and is unmemorable. Instead, get people's attention and share gratitude to your host or hosting organization a bit later.

3. **A long self-introduction read by an emcee or person introducing you:** Keep your list of qualifications focused and relatively short—no more than a few minutes. In fact, two to three minutes are probably plenty. Audiences need to know enough about you to listen, yet not so much that they lose interest.

4. **An attempt at opening with a joke (Karia, 2012):** Humor is great. A stale joke, however, is not. This type of introduction can miss the mark on so many levels. First, most people are lousy joke-tellers. If you don't clearly know your audience and the invisible boundaries of appropriateness, most jokes will lack the luster you hope to surface. Remember, your audience members did not sign up for a comedy club routine; they expect you to be professional, knowledgeable, and engaging. A joke will virtually always offend someone in the room—that is what makes it funny. Yet, this is not what your audience came to hear. Instead, jokes detract from your message. They are not worth the risk.

Introduction to Your Topic and Processes

As important as your informal and formal introductions of yourself are, equally important is the way you introduce the topic at hand. Some presenters may merge this into the formal introduction of themselves, while others will transition from their own information to the theme. Whichever you choose, be deliberate and make that transition smoothly.

Introduce the Topic

Introduce the topic both inductively and deductively. In other words, be sure to provide enough of the big picture to give those who need to see it a map of where your presentation is headed. Additionally, share the specific goals and objectives you will address in your presentation somewhere within the introduction to the matter. Both big-picture and specific components are important.

Introduce the Processes

Plan for purposeful group interaction. Group participants and explain the processes. Do you want the audience members to interact with one another? How? Decide that ahead of time, and infuse these groupings as part of the way in which you'll provide reflection about the subject matter. When you introduce your processes, you are essentially introducing to the audience members how they will have voice and opportunities for participation. Will you use small partner groups, table teams, or large-group interactions? Name the groups and provide a visual cue that will help them know what to do when they see it. Consistently reference the groups—don't call them shoulder partners one minute and seatmates the next. It is important to note that groupings should be natural and relatively easy to configure.

Consider adding a visual icon on your slides for each grouping or discussion reflection opportunity. For instance, use a picture of a team for the table team conversation, use a picture of a partner group for the elbow or shoulder partner conversation, and use a picture of a solo thinker for the time you want your audience to simply pause and reflect independently. These pictures or icons will connect your processes for discourse with the content delivery. This creates a flow between presenting and audience deliberation.

Use Openers

A great way to introduce the groupings as well as the content is to have each group of participants discuss or explore an opener or teaser to the presentation content. Openers are operational energizers. You want your audience to feel that something will be different from the typical, lackluster meetings they attend. If you do this subtly, adult audiences will respond with surprise and appreciation. Openers often reduce tension and anxieties, add a bit of energy into the room, and set a tone for involvement.

If you are speaking about leadership, ask the members of your table team to introduce themselves, and then discuss the qualities of great leaders they know. This way, you are getting your audience members to know one another, all the while warming their brains to the topic at hand. Another effective opener is to have your teams conduct a strategy like Stump Your Team (also known as Two Truths and a Lie), in which you tell the participants two true things about you along with one that is made up, and they must decide which is the lie. Another might simply be finding something a small group has in common that starts with the same letter of the alphabet. For instance, maybe all group members agree they like pizza. Although openers can sometimes feel a bit silly at first, they invite your participants to get their own voices into the room in a positive manner. When that happens, a remarkable byproduct occurs—you feel more comfortable and relaxed. There are a variety of suggestions and resources you can locate and use (see, for example, Duarte, 2012; Jensen, 1998; Solem & Pike, 1997).

Use Schedules and Norms of Operation

Humans work more efficiently and effectively when there are reasonable, adult-centered schedules and boundaries. Everyone wants to know how the day will play out, as most people are managing a myriad of responsibilities outside of your training. By sharing a schedule, your audience can anticipate breaks, lunch, and ending times, and in order to monitor times throughout the day, participants can check devices and their other obligations. Simply by sharing a schedule, you demonstrate to your audience members that you respect them and their time.

Introduce a limited set of norms to which you expect your audience will abide. These include things like how and when to ask questions, simple kindness toward one another, and following your requests for participation. Ways to introduce such norms include, but are not limited to, the following phrases.

- "Please abide by the attention signal."
- "Take care of your personal needs."
- "Monitor your time at breaks and lunch."
- "Please limit your technology use to breaks."
- "Enjoy your day!"

Employ a succinct yet kind (maybe even humorous) approach to delivering norms. I find that by doing this up front, you mitigate possible issues later on.

An Emphatic Conclusion

Just as openers infuse early energy into the room, closers tie things together. A good closer helps you revisit the key content and helps your audience leave with actions. Participants might practice what they learned, create a plan for using the information in the near future, or share a key learning. Often, closers function as a celebration of your time together and formally close your training session.

Novice presenters often run out of time, and the training is left with an abrupt stop. They may even say something like, "We're out of time, so I'll let you go," "Thank you," or, "Now that we're finished, please complete the evaluation. See you!" Instead of these clearly ineffective conclusions, I suggest you have two or three closure activities you can reference and use. Consider one that lasts ten to fifteen minutes, one that is three to five minutes, and maybe one that is only one to two minutes in length. Add these into the end of your presentation, and use whichever you have time to include. This way, you have a more thoughtful ending. Think of it like putting punctuation at the end of a sentence. Without it, the audience is left floundering a bit, and the training, no matter how great it has been, is now rushed with a curt closing. Your audience is left without opportunities to celebrate their learning, with nothing to reinforce some of their key learnings, or with a last impression that feels discombobulated (Solem, 1997).

Plan your ending virtually as much as you plan your introduction. An encapsulating quote, a perfect embedded video, or simply a heartfelt story can perfectly end an effective presentation. It doesn't need to be long—three to five minutes. Be certain it culminates the learning and leaves your audience inspired. As with opening ideas, there are also great print and web resources dedicated to closings in some of the same materials and from some of the same authors listed previously (for example, Pike, 1994; Solem & Pike, 1997).

Summary

In this section, I explored *what to do* and *what not to do* when beginning a presentation and introducing yourself and your topic. I also emphasized the importance of a strong conclusion. The next part of this resource details the components of a dynamic delivery.

Chapter 5

Delivering Your Message

*The human brain is a wonderful organ. It starts
to work as soon as you are born and doesn't stop
until you get up to deliver a speech.*

—George Jessel

You've planned your message, aligned it to the intended outcomes, and set the physical stage. It is now time to dynamically deliver your message. In this chapter, I highlight the components of getting your group's attention, using your voice effectively, and engaging with your participants using appropriate behaviors.

Getting the Group's Attention

Get your group's full attention before you speak. This aspect is critical! Do not speak to a group of adults without them attending to you. Getting attention prior to speaking does a couple of key things. One is quite obvious—it allows everyone to hear your information, and it likely saves twenty individual questions later. A more implicit reason is that it sends a subtle message that you are in control of the room. Audiences actually want to be assured of that. They need to know that someone in the room is in control. They may not outwardly tell you they need it, but they need to know they are safe—that respectful behaviors are expected and monitored, and that someone in the space is the leader. Consider using a phrase like "May I ask you to rejoin us?" or "Please pause your conversations." Both phrases indicate that you need participants' attention at this time, and that you are kindly asking for it. Yet, they also imply the group members don't have to completely *stop* what they are doing forever. Instead, they will pause to give you attention and later can complete conversations. This is important for adult audiences. Remember, what they have to say is important, too. Those collegial phrases subtly honor your participants while asking them to cease their current conversations.

Using Your Voice Effectively

Your voice is your presentation instrument. Warm it up, use it effectively, and treat it kindly. Pay attention to how you signify emphasis throughout your message. Ensure variation. Next, I provide tips for speaking articulately and showing passion, speaking clearly and powerfully, using your voice effectively, and displaying appropriate presenter behaviors.

Speak Articulately and Show Passion

Speak intelligently. As you reflect on your presentations, notice how your planned message compares to your delivered one. Be mindful of slang and shortened words, like *yeah*, *kinda*, and *sorta*, and expunge them from your vocabulary! You don't need to sound like a thesaurus, but you do need to show a strong command and use of language.

Share your message passionately. An audience perceives and appreciates presenters who really care about their topic. Your use of inflection and your word choice highlight that passion. Nevertheless, a speaker who is overly energetic for the entire time tires an audience. Conversely, a speaker who has limited inflection and inspiration will bore the audience. Write out much of what you want to say and rehearse it regularly, in order to deliver it well.

Speak Clearly and Powerfully

Voice dramatically affects audiences. Listen to your voice. Begin by simply standing and delivering your introduction. Is your voice rich and formidable? Is it too forceful and loud? Is it too high-pitched? Our voices naturally rise as we get nervous, in some cases by an octave. A high-pitched, shrill voice in a microphone can sound like nails on a chalkboard, a hurdle your audience will not be able to get over. To avoid this, practice. Ensure that your breathing is deep and filling up your lungs—that it is more diaphragmatic. This naturally enhances your pitch and allows your voice to be powerful in all ranges. A good strategy is to hold out your finger one foot in front of your mouth. Then pretend you are blowing out a candle. That feeling and that breath intensity is the one you want to use while presenting.

Attend to relaxing your shoulders and throat, straightening your posture, and breathing deeply as you begin (Blair, 2018). If you haven't done so already, read about or even get voice coaching from a trained speech therapist or pathologist. You will learn great warm-up strategies, pitch perfection, and the importance of using your voice without straining it. Does your voice strain easily? If your voice often feels tired or sounds hoarse after a presentation, you may need support in using your voice more appropriately. Be mindful that your vocal folds need rest after much use. If you speak all day, then exert your voice to speak with clients over a loud restaurant at dinner, your voice will pay an enormous price. Take care of the most important tool in your presenter toolbox, your voice. To do so, simply do not speak for awhile. Voice rest is the single fastest way to help your voice recover. Eliminate caffeinated and carbonated beverages, and opt for calming teas like chamomile or a tea called *throat coat*. Be certain you also have moisture in the room where you sleep. Dry air exacerbates voice problems. These suggestions seem so straightforward, and yet so many speakers never really hear themselves speak. Do so.

Enunciate. Articulate without overemphasizing. Some presenters overdo their consonants, so be careful. You want to be certain that you are understood, yet your voice sounds natural. If you have awkward words or phrases to say, something like "sound specificity" or "Heflebower," be certain you say it aloud many times, articulating and enunciating the words and phrases clearly. Do so in a microphone, and practice in a location where it echoes.

Pace Well

Another important use of sound is pacing. You want your words and phrases to flow with ease. The pause is an important component of sound pacing. The pause is powerful in emphasis, in using humor effectively, and in providing thoughtful reflection. It means you must be content with silence. Allow your words to land. Let there be some silence occasionally, as it provides variation and impact. We all know the importance of the pause after a comment intending humor. It takes a few seconds for the audience to hear your words and react. Let that happen. Be mindful that the larger the room and the more the acoustics perpetuate echoing, your pausing will be more often intentional, and your pacing will need to slow.

Nerves impede your pacing. You may find that you speed up your rate of speech dramatically and unknowingly when you get in front of an audience of any size! One strategy to help is simply to think about using more pauses. Allow some silence in between your phrases and sentences. Also, apply breathing techniques, maybe even placing your hand on your stomach or diaphragm to remind you.

Avoid Filler Words

Filler words—*um, uh, well, yeah, like, so,* and so on—are the kiss of death. They truly alienate your audience immediately. Why? Because we all remember our required speech group and its emphasis on deleting filler words from our vocabulary. We expect presenters to refrain from using filler words, period. These are prevalent in casual conversation, yet simply cannot be part of your professional speaking vocabulary. As Christopher Bell, a communications professor at the University of Colorado Colorado Springs, said during college freshman orientation, "Nothing intelligent follows three 'likes'" (C. Bell, personal communication, August 16, 2018). If you aren't sure about your own speaking habits, ask friends or colleagues. They know. Use a helpful app such as LikeSo. This app listens to you speak, counts your filler words, and reports them. What useful and unobtrusive tools to help you perfect the sound of silence! Ensure you monitor your filler words during all aspects of your presentation. You might become skilled at avoiding these words during your formal presentation, yet realize they creep back in when you are taking questions or doing something a bit more off the cuff. Remember to listen, pause, think, and then answer. Confident and competent speakers are comfortable with periods of silence. No filler words are needed. They are simply distracting.

Watch Up-Speak

In addition to unconscious speaking slang, some presenters exercise *up-speak* (DiResta, 2019). This is the notion of ending many of your sentences in an upward sound. Some even add up-speak terms, such as "Right?," "Make sense?," and "Okay?" All of these lessen your credibility. Instead, end directions or requests in a down-tone—when your voice actually drops in sound. For example, "Please be seated," Thank you," and "Please react to this idea" all end in a down-tone. This sounds more authoritative and confident. When you raise your voice at the end of the sentence, it makes what you say sound optional or uncertain. Practice this a bit. Say a few words—even your name. Do you naturally end upward or downward? Check yourself, and monitor your up-speak accordingly.

Displaying Appropriate Presenter Behaviors

Your presentation meshes both presenter behaviors and your message. The two together, when exercised well, are a perfect union. However, a strong message with limited presenting delivery behaviors leaves participants disappointed. Often the members of an audience revere a well-known author, one whose work they have read for years, and attend a session with high hopes, only to leave dissatisfied because the famous writer ineffectively shared his or her work. Conversely, a presenter with only strong presenting skills leaves an audience feeling hollow if there is not a corresponding, compelling, and content-related message. Skilled presenters master *both*.

Have Presence

When you walk into a room, what do others think? How do they perceive you? Watch. Notice. These are important considerations worth perceiving. If people turn their heads a bit, give you eye contact, and engage in conversation, you have presence. You want that as a presenter. You should be noticed and in a positive way.

How do you walk? Videotape yourself in order to observe your movement patterns and tendencies. You want to walk confidently with straight posture, stomach held tight, and leading your gait heel to toe. If you slouch, clomp your feet, or have awkward movement patterns, over half of your audience will judge you accordingly—most likely negatively. Small things matter when audiences are visually summing up a presenter. Your audience members will likely watch whether or not you interacted with guests or if you were more standoffish and will form a tentative opinion about you before you ever open your mouth. They notice everything—your attire, your accessories, and, of course, your presence. In fact, Michael Solomon (in Solomon, Hughes, Chitty, Marshall, & Stuart, 2005), a psychologist at New York University, coined the *7-11 rule*, which estimated that people make eleven decisions about you within the first seven seconds of meeting you that can forever shape the nature of the relationship. Even if your audience makes only three decisions about you, ensure these decisions are favorable. If you need support, a resource I recommend is *Brilliant Body Language* by Max A. Eggert (2010).

Mind Your Attire

Be mindful of your attire and the image it portrays. You can certainly be stylish *and* professional. Gentlemen, read about the types of jackets, shirt collars, and ties that enhance your body type. One big mistake men make is that their clothes do not fit. They may have fit a year before, or the last time he put on that jacket, yet they don't fit now. The shirt might pull and not allow a male presenter to move his arms freely. His pants may be too long or too short, or he might suffer the telltale faux pas—the suit jacket sleeves are too long. If people are going to give up time and often money to see you, care enough to tailor your clothing appropriately. Ladies, pay very close attention to this. A presentation should not serve as your first chance to walk from *Vogue* magazine. If in doubt, be more conservative in your dress and add more stylish accessories—a fun bracelet, scarf, or pair of shoes. Dress a bit more formally than your audience. Ensure your shoes are polished and fashionable, yet practical. Often you are standing or moving on a stage, tile, or low-pile carpet floor that may hurt your feet and legs over time. Be certain your attire is professional, fits you well, and is comfortable.

Portray Confidence

Be confident, but never arrogant. A presenter exuding confidence is poised and knowledgeable. Yet, he or she is considerate and remembers that he or she is a continual learner in the field. Too many presenters teeter into overconfidence, and an audience will perceive that immediately. Arrogant presenters truly convey they are the best, and that no one knows as much or is as good as they. Never let yourself dip into that abyss. You should be assured, self-reliant, and courageous to do this work well; otherwise, everyone could and would do it. Nevertheless, refrain emphatically from superiority. And remember, perceiving haughtiness is an audience's decision. You may not intend to have such a persona, but if even one audience member senses your arrogance, you have lost. Period. I have watched haughtiness ruin otherwise exceptional presenters—those I thought were at the pinnacle in their field, only to listen to audience comments and watch colleagues roll their eyes about the presenter's inflated ego. Appreciate positive feedback, but never, ever let it go to your head.

Engage Me, Don't Irritate Me

Audiences want to be engaged. Adult audiences don't want to do childish activities about which they see no point. For example, don't break into a silly song, expecting participants to sing along, if they're not really into the training. Now, that does not mean that you need to always be serious and avoid all childlike moments, but childlike is different from childish. Instead, use adult-centered activities that will be engaging. I include some examples for engagement in the next sections.

Use Humor

Adults appreciate a sense of humor. In fact, it will connect an audience to you and the content faster than most other tactics. Yet, the humor should always be self-deprecating and appropriate. Using humor is not telling a joke. Jokes are when you are making fun of someone or a group. Humor is a funny story, a catchy phrase, or the use of idioms and metaphors. Humor is not directed toward anyone, except possibly yourself.

What adults find humorous runs the gamut. Be cautious and realize that "comedy show humor" works with late-night crowds who may have imbibed adult beverages. It won't work with professional audiences. One wrong move with humor can derail the entire presentation. Like the familiar saying spoken by Margaret Wolfe Hungerford (Wikipedia, n.d.), "Beauty is in the eye of the beholder." Well, humor is in the brain of the beholder. It is important to consider the humor you want to insert and try it out first with a few different groups—maybe a dinner party or a small group of friends. Do so when and where the audience is small so that if it goes a bit awry or is insulting, the audience is small and didn't pay to see you! If you're confident the humor is working, try it out for a larger presentation or two. If the audience doesn't respond, drop it like a bad habit. You may have heard it said, "If in doubt, leave it out." Do not go too far to the fringes in using your humor. A funny story or a set of silly pictures that connect your ideas might be a great place to start.

The key to using humor is understanding and using the power of the pause (P. Gordon, personal communication, November 1, 2011). Humor needs to land. It needs time and space in the room to be effective. Sarcasm is but one mode of effective, adult humor. Yet, again, it needs to be used tactfully, and not at the expense of others in the room.

Video clips inserted at the perfect moment can provide an element of humor. In fact, using videos (for which you have obtained permission) often adds humor into the room indirectly. It is a safer way to start. Presenters who are not naturally funny may want to embed a few humorous quotes or videos. The audience laughter actually settles most presenters and puts them a bit more at ease.

In most cases, humor comes as a risk worth taking. Where a joke during an intro is typically ineffective, use of humor at an appropriate point in the presentation often is effective. Be mindful—an honest attempt to infuse humor is often not only appreciated, but also celebrated by the masses. Yet, a few participants may find it offensive. It is a topic for your reflection. If you find that most people laugh at your humor during conversations, gatherings, and impromptu conversations, you are skilled at infusing humor. If, however, most of your closest friends wouldn't consider you funny, then use it sparingly at first. Add it into places for an effect. Over time, you may find you can introduce it more naturally into the conversation of your presentation.

Connect Naturally

Audiences are people. People crave connections. So, a great presenter must connect with audience members—no matter how many are in the room. One way to connect is to ensure you obtain and maintain eye contact with individuals. Everyone in the room notices when the presenter doesn't look at people. It's awkward, plain and simple. So, begin by scanning the first few rows. Allow your eyes to pan the room, pausing at about every fourth or fifth person. As you pause momentarily, look at them. Connect with them. Then, continue that strategy as you gradually move your gaze left, middle, right, front, back, outside edges, inside edges, all over the room. You would hope to look everyone in the eye throughout a session lasting a few hours. Your audience will know and notice. Alternatively, you may choose the old tactic shared in speech group called *look above*. This self-explanatory strategy allows you to look just above the heads of your audience members in order to stifle nervousness. But to a large audience, it will still appear as though you are maintaining eye contact.

Summary

After you have carefully planned your message, connected it to the intended outcomes, and ensured the room was arranged appropriately, you should focus on your delivery. In this chapter, I highlighted the components of getting your group's attention, using your voice effectively and powerfully, and engaging with your participants using appropriate presenter behaviors. The next chapter will emphasize the print and visual portion of your presentations.

Chapter 6

Designing Visuals and Print Materials

We are visual creatures. Visual things stay put,
whereas sounds fade.

—Steven Pinker

Strong visuals and print materials augment your message. Some presenters go without either. Others rely heavily on both. Whichever your message and your style, gravitate toward what is right for you. Using these materials meritoriously is key. In this chapter, I discuss the effective use of visual enhancements and handouts, as well as considerations for presenting in a visual medium, such as via webinar.

Visual Enhancements

Although some presenters (mostly keynoters) are quite successful without using any form of visual support, most aren't. Remember that using multiple modalities (auditory, visual, and kinesthetic) better cements learning in the brain (University of Pennsylvania, 2009). As Sheryl Feinstein (2006) states, "The visual sense is arguably the most powerful way that the brain gathers information about the environment, and the processing of visual data and its resulting images is intimately and essentially linked to learning and cognition" (p. 491). In fact, Allen (2008) reiterates that point when he concludes,

> *Maximizing the visual field means attending to the total training environment, including walls, bulletin boards, ceilings, and windows, using props, displays, images, and posters. When we use our entire teaching*

stage, our training becomes akin to a surround-sound experience, advancing learning to a new level. (p. 106)

Therefore, by using well-planned visuals, you can better ensure your audience remembers your message.

Visuals to Plan Your Message Thoughtfully

Be certain you have considered your audience size, the type of training you are conducting (keynote versus training, for instance), and your content options (see chapter 2, page 15). These considerations will naturally drive the amount of visual support you need.

Some presenters suggest brainstorming your key and supporting ideas first by placing one idea on a sticky note. Often, when you design using presentation software, the linear nature of such software programs—one slide after another—may actually stifle your thinking and planning. However, arranging and rearranging sticky notes can help you establish your thinking. Break your big ideas into little ones, and arrange them into a logical order that makes sense to you as the presenter, as well as to the audience. After clearly laying out your ideas, move them into visual formats. You might recall the sticky note strategy described previously. This is one way to move your ideas into groups and categories so you can begin to see the natural visual layout.

Presentation Software Tips

One visual format is presentation software. Although it has a bit of a bad rap (recall the oft-heard phrase, "Death by PowerPoint"), such software is designed to enhance presentations and provides effective visual support. I'm often asked my preferences among the most common software options (Google Slides, Microsoft PowerPoint, Keynote, and Prezi), and I respond with PowerPoint for a number of reasons. First, you don't have to have internet connectivity to use it. Second, it is still the most common software program and can more easily be shared with others using either PC or Mac platforms, whereas Keynote software is not readily available on non-Mac platforms. Instead, it requires more steps to transform into a more common format like PowerPoint. However, Prezi and Google Slides offer some attractive visual options that are more limited than PowerPoint. Whatever your preference, get comfortable with your software and learn how to use its many features.

As you place your brainstormed ideas onto the slides, remember a few key slide development ideas.

- Put only the main points on a slide. Keep your notes and smaller details in the notes section for your reference.

- Place no more than six lines of text on a slide.

- Use a minimum of twenty-four-point font, yet be mindful of the room size. You may need a larger font size.

- Use only one or two font styles. You don't want to confuse your audience with various fonts.

- Ensure that font style, color, and size are consistent and easily read. Look at your slides from afar. Some fonts are more easily noticed than others. Stick with Times or Arial variations if in doubt.

- Bring your slides to life with pictures, not clip art.

- Use animation sparingly. Avoid distracting or annoying your audience with sound or transitions that may make audience members motion sick.

- Embed video and audio clips. Be certain you know where they are coming in your presentation. Some presenters insert a black screen as a reminder that a video is upcoming. It allows you to set it up and not surprise your audience with an irrelevant clip.

Paying attention to slide design details makes you a more elite presenter.

Editing Tips

When reviewing the visual you create, try to see your work as a participant would. Be certain you review your work a number of times. Someone once told me to review my message one time for as many people as there would be in my audience. Therefore, I would review it fifty times for an audience size of fifty participants. Although that seems excessive, the point is that you cannot review your message enough. You will most assuredly find conventional errors in grammar, spelling, capitalization, and the like, every time you review.

Ensure you check your work carefully not only for spelling mistakes and grammatical errors, but also for how your message flows. Try to run through your message as though you were learning it for the first time. Does everything make sense? Ensure all the terms are defined adequately so everyone can understand. Additionally, know your work and the order of your slides well enough to be able to present without referencing your software slides. Finally, refrain from reading the content on your slides. As Karia (2017) states, "If you and your PowerPoint are saying the same thing, one of you is not needed" (p. 141).

Handout Design

A supportive handout truly strengthens a strong presentation. You want handouts to supplement your message, not supplant it. If your handout contains everything you are discussing, why would your audience need to listen? Instead, allow your handout to provide active responses to key questions, or places for participants to take notes. This helps deepen their understanding of your content and presentation ideas.

Add details to help your audience follow along. One important feature is to ensure your handout is paginated. I like to add a picture of the handout slide with the corresponding page to my visual presentation slides. This allows audience members to easily know if there is an equivalent handout page or whether they need to take their own notes. It simply makes following along with a handout easier. Another feature is about where to place your biographical information. If you print a biography, consider adding it at the end of your handout instead of the beginning of it. This makes your audience realize the training isn't about *you*. One more tip is to provide blank notes pages at the back of your handout, as well as any activity sheets the audience will reference often.

Although this should go without much discussion, be certain you have obtained the rights to share printed, visual, or embedded video information. If you are in doubt, check the many online sources, like the Copyright Clearance Center (www.copyright.com), to help you. Plan ahead, as your request may take a few days to a few weeks for a response from the author or copyright holder.

Presentations via Webinar

Presentations are done in various environments. A common one today is using some form of webinar software from a remote location. Although this is a great convenience for a presenter, since you don't have to travel to your site, you do give up the personal factor you obtain onsite. I often encourage presenters to use web formats as a follow-up instrument, rather than a first training opportunity. In order for a webinar to be successful, internet connectivity at all sites joining the conference via webinar is critical. Be certain to test this out prior to contracting the webinar, as well as fifteen to thirty minutes prior to the start of the session.

Webinars can be effective and cost-efficient when done properly. The following are a few checks for consideration.

- Check your lighting. Will it stay the same throughout the presentation time? Do you have shadows or glares that might impede the camera? Review to ensure shine on faces or glasses isn't distracting.

- Check your background for pictures, books, or other items. Ensure your setting is professional.

- Be sure all pets and children are contained. No one needs to see a cat slithering around your desk, or a child sneaking in!

- Account for ancillary sounds (doorbells, air conditioner, heaters, fans, neighborhood noises, and so on).

- Ensure your computer is secure and the angle stays consistent.

- Attend to your eye and body movements. Is your camera located in a place you will easily look into, or will you be referencing something where your gaze will drift regularly? Will your gestures enhance the presentation and be seen? Will they be cut off?

- Check the sound in both directions. Can you easily hear those on the other end? Do you need to use headphones? Would an additional speaker assist? Can you also be heard well on the receiving side?

- Check your comforts. Is the temperature okay? Will your face flush if you close the door and it gets too hot? Do you need water to drink?

- Mute participants not speaking. Any noises will be picked up and will be distracting. Think someone keyboarding—that will be heard!

- Use video as long as it will be seen and heard without delays. It is a good way to add a mode change, yet needs to be considered useful, not distracting.

- Be certain you know, and can use, all of the tools in the webinar software platform. Will you take questions? Can you effectively use the chat boxes or questioning options?

Webinars offer a useful follow-up or question-and-answer platform for attendees. They are less expensive, and can be very helpful in highlighting a specific detail or component of your message. If you attend to the aforementioned suggestions, webinars will serve as an additional and effective learning mode.

Summary

Throughout this chapter, I concentrated on the various considerations for delivering your message more dynamically. These included effective visual enhancements and handouts, and strategies for solid webinars and facilitated sessions. Strong presentation delivery is arduous. Yet, delivering your message dynamically makes a huge difference. The following chapter discusses the next critical step in perfecting your message: reflecting on your presentation.

Chapter 7

Reflecting on Your Practice

Time spent in self-reflection is never wasted—it is an intimate date with yourself.

—Paul T. P. Wong

After planning your message and drawing together all your hard work, you delivered your message. How did it go? How do you know—really? You want to be certain you obtain feedback and reflect on that from a myriad of reputable sources. Such reflection will help you hone your craft for future trainings.

Obtaining quality feedback from your audiences is vital. It should be specific, timely, the right amount, and understandable. Feedback is an essential part of the learning process and, done well, has notable impact. Hattie (2009) defines feedback as "information provided by an agent (e.g., audience, colleague, or one's own experience) about aspects on one's performance or understanding" (p. 174). Effective feedback is information provided to complement, enhance, augment, or in some way respond to or improve performance. In this chapter, I highlight why feedback and reflective practice are so important, introduce practical methods for obtaining honest and helpful responses, and present ideas for using the information for improving your practice.

The Importance of Reflective Practice

Robert J. Marzano (2012) states, "Reflective practice is highly esteemed and widely used in many professions, especially those that require on-the-spot decisions and adaptations" (p. 4). Presenting to adults demands careful reflection. You should always be thinking, monitoring, adjusting, and refining as you present—much like teaching participants. Simply put, reflecting on your practice makes you a better professional speaker. There will be times when your keynote, training, or facilitated session simply bombs. That is part of the territory. Just like I described in the introduction to this book, it is a matter not of *if* you fail, but of *when*. Consequently, your timely and honest reflection will be the difference between obtaining a level of mediocrity or achieving one of greatness.

Debunk the myth right now that talent or innate abilities separate competent from incompetent presenters. Sure, it helps if you can overcome some of the basic necessities in working with adults—conquering debilitating nerves, organizing content, and speaking eloquently—but those skills are only the beginning.

Great presenters work at being great presenters. K. Anders Ericsson, Ralf T. Krampe, and Clemens Tesch-Römer (1993) state, "The differences between expert performers and normal adults reflect a life-long period of deliberate effort to improve performance" (p. 400). In fact, Ericsson et al. (1993) went on to coin the phrase *deliberate practice*. Using deliberate practice means that you use feedback and diligently focus your efforts on specific areas in which you want to improve. It is not just the mere notion of practicing, but practicing with purpose. As Marzano (2012) states, "Deliberate practice also requires large amounts of time" (p. 7). It takes perseverance to hone a presenter's craft. Mihaly Csikszentmihalyi, Kevin Rathunde, and Samuel Whalen (1993) likewise state, "Unless a person wants to pursue the difficult path that leads to the development of talent, neither innate potential nor all the knowledge in the world will suffice" (pp. 31–32). You must *want* to improve. Although such a desire might seem universal, the arrogant presenter (noted in chapter 5, page 45) does not possess this. Continual deliberate practice helps the brain develop stronger systems of remembering, organizing, and using new information in future situations.

Categories of Feedback

Research on feedback dates back to the early 1900s with Thorndike's (1913) writing about positive reinforcement and negative feedback. Other researchers (Bangert-Drowns, Kulik, Kulik, & Morgan, 1991; Butler & Winne, 1995; Hattie & Timperley, 2007; Kluger & DeNisi, 1996) were instrumental in adding to the collective body of research. These authors shared the significance of learners obtaining and using feedback to further learning. Let's translate that into presenting: presenters who regularly obtain accurate and useful information about their performances increase their effectiveness.

Among the research, there are different categories of feedback. They include task, processing, self-regulation, and generalizations about the person (Brookhart, 2017).

- *Task feedback* relates to whether or not there is correctness in the completed task itself. Did you achieve the training outcomes you intended?

- *Feedback about processing* assesses strategies the presenter used or may have considered when actually doing a task. What activities did you use? Were they effective? Will you use or modify them in future presentations?

- *Self-regulation feedback* involves presenters evaluating themselves and their confidence with a task or process.

- Finally, *generalizations about the person* are namely that—how "good," "bad," "thorough," or "thoughtful" a presenter may appear. These are statements that generalize the specific feedback into more overarching descriptors (Hattie & Timperley, 2007).

Feedback that recognizes the processes and quality of work, as well as that related to self-regulation, tends to be the most influential to improving a presenter's craft. That makes logical sense. Feedback that is inherent to something within the presenter's control fosters more self-efficacy and long-term improvement. The rationale is simple—when presenters think they can control an outcome, they are more vested in making change happen. They will put forth the effort. Brookhart (2008) captures this when she emphasizes, "Feedback about the person ('smart girl!') is generally not a good idea . . . feedback about the person can contribute to participants believing that intelligence is fixed. This implies that achievement is something beyond the participant's control" (p. 21). Again, let us transfer this to the context of presenting. Consider yourself the participant. When you gain universal or vague feedback about your work, it is inherently less helpful.

Considerations for Obtaining Quality Feedback

Acquiring feedback can be a complex endeavor. What is a presenter to do? In reviewing the literature, a number of resources identify various components that make feedback of higher quality and useful to the recipient (Brookhart, 2008; Butler & Nisan, 1986; Carless, 2006; Dweck, 2007; Hattie, 2009; Hattie & Timperley, 2007; Kluger & DeNisi, 1996; Marzano & Haystead, 2008; Nuthall, 2005). The following list includes a culmination of characteristics for quality feedback. It should be:

- Clear

- Specific

- Timely

- Relevant

- The right amount

- Focused on the task, the process, and self-monitoring

For our purposes, we will focus on only a few of these characteristics—specificity, timeliness, and amount. These components are summarized with clarity, suggestions, and examples throughout this section.

Specificity

Specificity relates to ensuring that feedback provides enough detail so you know what to celebrate or improve. For example, after a presentation, you may receive feedback that says, "Good job." Although you may initially feel pleased, you are left feeling a bit void. More specific (and useful) feedback might include, "I appreciate how you outlined your topic examples in logical order." Therefore, you must create feedback tools to obtain the specificity that will help you learn and improve. Jonathon Saphier (2005) states the importance of gaining just enough feedback to get yourself redirected or moving ahead. The feedback you seek and obtain should be specific in detail and suggestions.

Create Evaluation or Feedback Tools

Create an evaluation or feedback tool to provide you with useful information. A few sample questions you may consider include the following.

- What was something shared that validated your existing practices?

- What did the presenter do to help you learn?

- What (specifically) could the presenter improve to help you learn better?

- How did the visual or print materials support the learning?

- What general comments (if any) would you share?

Although these are only a few examples, they are good ones. They seek feedback from your audience that will help you improve. They are specific, yet succinct. Participants do not want to spend many minutes providing you feedback. So, focus your questions. First, ask yourself what you want to know. Then, ensure your evaluation tool asks those types of specific questions. For example, if you want to know if you were engaging, then ask, "What strategies did the presenter use that engaged you as a learner?" If you want feedback about the handout, say something like, "Tell me about the effectiveness of the handout used." Ask about that which you want to know, and reflect.

I am commonly asked, "Should I use the same evaluation tool for every presentation I provide?" My advice is to be *very cautious* about using a blanket evaluation tool for every training session. While this may provide you with some consistent data over time, it is often useless and irrelevant. For example, if you have a canned evaluation tool that asks the same questions of every audience, it may or may not relate to the type of presentation you conducted. If you facilitated a group discussion and there was not a handout, then asking about the print materials is inappropriate. If you had an informal meeting with a small team, asking about the activities and engagement may, again, be unconnected. Consequently, using data without the presenting context often invalidates it. Seek information that will be useful and valued. Don't waste your audience's time—or yours, for that matter—completing a replicated evaluation tool that doesn't relate in format or content to the training you painstakingly created and presented. Evaluation tools must be authentic. One more suggestion: explain to your audience how you will see and plan to use the results you obtain. This will likely increase participants' desire to complete feedback tools, and their honesty in so doing. When people know how you will use the results, they are more inclined to care.

Utilize Comments

Evaluation tools may provide both quantitative (numbers or averaged values) and qualitative (comments and observations) information. Both can be useful. Some evaluation tools contain some type of Likert scale about which participants rate their agreement as they respond to attitudinal statements (Likert, 1932). When using this scale for presentation evaluations, you will most commonly ask participants to check boxes or circle a number on a scale from 1 to 4 or 1 to 5 to indicate levels of your performance, much like an online Google rating for a business or service provider. This type of quantitative result may be helpful if the goal is quantifying numbers for your comparison to yourself previously, or to others. Sometimes that is important. Examples might include quantifying numbers for a federal or state grant, or comparing topics from a district perspective for funding future offerings.

Yet, a simple averaged value will only give you a general sense of useful information—a place to start. In addition to the Likert averages, I always like to include space for comments below the online ratings, and then I reference the comments to gain insights into the rankings. This makes the numbers come to life. If common, repeated statements are noted, it strengthens the results. It provides you with a qualitative theme, useful in making detailed changes. So, a Likert-averaged value may provide you with a quick glance at your effectiveness, but it has significant limitations. A single number hardly represents specificity. Be mindful, and always seek and reference comments to support the numbers. That will provide you with the specifics you need to make necessary adjustments.

Be Mindful of Comparisons

Quantitative values naturally impose comparative perspectives. It's simply the nature of the data. Comparisons are somewhat helpful when you desire to see your relative value compared to other presenters. However, it can also be a debilitating trap when a novice speaker overemphasizes such data. One negative evaluative number can skew an average and send you reeling. To add insult to injury, you may not have the context about which the number was generated. Such data can have a negative impact without providing any identifiable ideas for improvement. More often, feedback comparing you to others is less useful to your overall improvement—especially as you mature in your speaking abilities. You may not know what other presenters the group had, the topics that were presented, the formats, and the like.

When comparing yourself to others, be mindful of many considerations. First, some topics are simply easier to present, as the nature of the topic promotes more instant buy-in from an audience. For instance, a motivational topic or a new, easy-to-implement instructional strategy is often met with ease by weary trainers or facilitators. Therefore, the audience may perceive these presentations as "better." Other topics, like grading practices, may be more controversial and invoke a philosophical shift for the participants.

These topics are equally, if not even more, important; however, audiences may perceive such provocative ideas as negative or even devalued, since their application requires more significant change and complicated shifts in thinking. Keeping this in perspective is key when comparing feedback among presenters. This is not to say that both types of training topics (philosophically easy or difficult) cannot be more or less effectively presented, but it is important for one's overall perception during reflection. Furthermore, comparative data in such situations are unfair. So, although Likert scales are more efficient for audiences to complete, they are only minimally helpful in obtaining specific feedback. Rather, seek specific comments that will tell you much more.

Feedback should not be limited to constructive comments and corrections. Rather, allow participants to provide specific comments on strengths as well. Knowing what works well with many participants will be as useful in helping you repeat the behavior as knowing what you might need to modify.

Timeliness

Obtain feedback from your organization and participants as soon as possible. If time permits, ask for responses upon the completion of the session, as such feedback will be fresh and relevant. The amount of time between the presentation session and the feedback you obtain has a critical effect on results. The longer you wait to obtain feedback, the less likely you are to get enough returned surveys to use in a meaningful way (Bangert-Drowns et al., 1991; Stronge, 2007). A good rule of thumb in qualitative research is minimally a 30 percent return rate. So, if you have one hundred participants, you should seek thirty survey responses in order to meet that 30 percent threshold and have enough data to use effectively. Anything less, and you may be getting extreme results, as opposed to a solid gauge of the session.

Using electronic reflective surveys can be timely. Consider the pros and cons of using them for reflective feedback. The pros include the fact that electronic feedback is sensible and convenient for most audiences who have immediate access to technology. Because of this immediacy, you may obtain well-timed responses about the training you just completed. Not only can you quickly get feedback, but also many of the electronic surveying instruments used will collate the results for you, so as to save you time when compiling information to see trends and patterns. The downside is that many people are bombarded with electronic surveys. They are asked to rate the grocery store, restaurants, flights, and many businesses they frequent. People may have survey fatigue. Additionally, you may get an increase in skewed results. Often people are more inclined to complete an electronic survey either when they are really satisfied or when they are not. You may only get the extreme responses I previously cautioned against.

Remember that you have a dichotomous purpose in obtaining timely information—you need to meet the needs of both your audience and the school or district that invited or hired you. Many times those are in alignment. Sometimes they are not. Consider how you will obtain feedback from the person who contacted and contracted with you. I strongly encourage you to check in with your host (principal or district leader) regularly.

I often confirm the plan of the day and the logistics upon arriving (even though you have discussed this during planning calls or written correspondences). At the first break, find your host and check in. Ask questions to guide you. I often ask the host, "Is everything going as you had hoped? Is there anything I need to do more or less of?" This provides you with a feeling about the host's satisfaction and also enables you to adjust early on, as needed. Check back in during lunch, during afternoon break, and at the end of the training session. If your host isn't happy, then likely others aren't either. Be mindful. Be aware. Adjust as needed.

Yet another essential characteristic of timeliness is ensuring that you make time *to actually react* to the feedback. This is especially important in working with long-term contracts. If there is no opportunity for you to make corrections or modify your work, the feedback is a missed opportunity. One important point noted by Boulet, Simard, and de Melo (1990) is to ensure that regardless of the type of feedback provided, presenters make time to react to it and use it for improvement. Using feedback allows you to make presentation corrections, with repetitive practice helping to ensure the new practice becomes permanent.

Novice presenters may approach evaluation results a bit differently than experienced presenters. As a novice presenter, consider deep reviews after every training session you conduct until you have presented the same topic and format a dozen or so times. This way, you are seeing and using feedback to make regular adjustments. You will begin to see patterns of what works well, and what you need to adjust. However, one cautionary note: wait twenty-four hours prior to reviewing the evaluations in a deep manner. Doing so accounts for a decrease in the emotional reaction you will naturally notice and provides you with a more objective perspective. The rationale is straightforward: our brains recognize anything potentially threatening and will immediately assert a downshifting of neurotransmitter energy from the prefrontal cortex, where thinking, decision making, and impulse control occur, to that of the limbic, or emotional, area of the brain (Feinstein, 2006). Simply put, you will read and respond to the results more rationally as you allow time in between the presentation and the review of results. This allows you to be more likely to receive critical feedback more objectively.

If you are a seasoned presenter, still make time for occasional feedback reviews. Although you will likely know your strength and challenge trends, you should review evaluation results, seeking more ways to fine-tune your strengths. You may also recognize some sloppy or poor habits you have developed over time that you need to attend to. For instance, maybe you have become less detailed with your print resources or the timing of your planning. Your goal is to make good great. Never settle for thinking you have arrived at the top. That is a dangerous perspective, even for a very experienced presenter. Consequently, you may begin to teeter into the realm of arrogance.

Allow yourself time to use the feedback you receive, and adjust your performance accordingly. In the next section (see page 66), I provide samples of reflective progressions to assist you in maximizing your time when reviewing survey results.

Amount

Select a couple of main components about which to obtain comments, rather than asking audiences to comment on everything. Think *triage* here. In an emergency room, the person with the most serious injury or illness will be assisted first. What is the most important content piece or skill about which you want feedback? Use a short survey with a few key questions. The one I use and like best asks the following.

- What specifically worked for you?

- What suggestions might you offer?

- On a scale of 1–4, with 1 being the lowest and 4 the highest, how would you rate this session?

- Do you have any other general comments?

A two- or more-page reflection feels cumbersome to the audience, and you may actually get fewer results and less interest in completing it. After a long day of training, participants are tired. Honor them by making your reflective survey manageable. Also, be sure you actually complete your own reflection survey prior to administering it, so you know how much time it will take most people. Tell your audience the approximate time it should take to complete. Say something like, "Your feedback is really important to my improvement. Please take two minutes of time to complete this simple survey and leave it on your tables as you leave."

Ideas for Improving Your Practice

The most important thing when seeking feedback is ultimately how you then use the feedback to improve your presentations. In this section, I will detail four different methods of reflection or feedback, along with how you can use them to continually improve your practice.

- Completing reflective progressions

- Conducting self-reflection

- Seeking help from a trusted colleague

- Using quality feedback for goal setting

Completing Reflective Progressions

One way to consider reflecting about your performance more specifically is to use a reflective progression. A reflective progression focuses on one facet of your presentation at a time and exemplifies levels of attainment. For instance, if you are focusing on an effective message, the reflective progression will provide descriptors for three levels— (1) below expectation, (2) at expectation, and (3) above expectation. Using reflective progressions assists you in reviewing and refining your levels of competency about various presenting processes and skills (Heflebower, 2005; Heritage, 2008; Marzano, 2006).

The following figures (figures 7.1, 7.2, 7.3, 7.4, 7.5, and 7.6, pages 67–68) are sample reflective progressions for the components of effective messaging, room arrangement, introductions, engagement, visual and print materials, and the conclusion.

Outstanding	Proficient	Developing
• You engaged each quadrant of the audience consistently throughout your message. • You incorporated connecting phrases like "Imagine this . . ." or "Here's how this might work" to transition from one quadrant to the next.	• It was evident you applied the audience member quadrant in planning your message. • There were examples for each type of participant throughout most of your key points.	• There was no clear key point development in your message. • You engaged one or two quadrant components, yet they didn't feel planned or had limited effectiveness.

Figure 7.1: Effective messaging.

Outstanding	Proficient	Developing
• You used the room to enhance your delivery. • The lighting, sound, and visuals provided an optimal learning environment. • There was a "wow" factor when participants entered the room.	• You arranged the room so all could see and hear easily. • You had pathways for yourself to move about the room. • Participants could move during your engaging activities. • The room and setup felt professional.	• The space stifled active engagement. • Participants looked or felt uncomfortable. • The audience may have struggled to see or hear you.

Figure 7.2: Room arrangement.

Outstanding	Proficient	Developing
• Your introduction evoked positive emotion from the group (laughter, smiles, or "aw" moments). • You set up your expectations flawlessly and infused your topic into those experiences.	• You used a planned introduction of yourself that lasted no more than three or four minutes. • You had an introduction to your topic. • You set up your groupings and audience processing opportunities.	• You allowed someone to read your biography to the group. • You didn't set up your processing options for the audience.

Figure 7.3: Introductions.

Outstanding	Proficient	Developing

• You used a variety of engagement strategies at just the right times.
• Participants showed obvious enjoyment.
	• You used a variety of engagement strategies:
	  • Music
	  • Activities
	  • Reflection
	  • Physical movement
	  • There were examples for each type of participant throughout most of your key points.
		• Your audience wavered in attentiveness.

Figure 7.4: Delivery—engagement.

Outstanding	Proficient	Developing
• Your handout was a perfect complement to the presentation. It didn't provide too much or too little. • Your visuals and slides incorporated high-quality pictures and graphics. • The handout encouraged interaction.	• Your print materials complemented the presentation. They included additions or examples. • Your visual charts and slides were easy to read. They had key information, but not too much text. • The handout included space for notes and applications of the content.	• Your print materials didn't complement the presentation (too much or too little). • Handout was difficult to follow (for example, no pagination, much flipping around, no place for notes). • Your visuals were difficult to read.

Figure 7.5: Delivery—visual and print materials.

Outstanding	Proficient	Developing
• Your conclusion didn't feel like a change in pace. There were no "Now we're concluding" phrases or moments. It flowed smoothly. You helped the audience see all they learned. • Your audience immediately denoted applications of many of the training components. • Your audience left with an inspirational, touching moment.	• You had an interactive and fun conclusion that incorporated the major components of the training. • Your audience left with at least one immediate next step.	• You had limited to no conclusion. • Participants never reflected on all of the content and processes addressed during the session.

Figure 7.6: Conclusion.

Conducting Self-Reflection

After completing the reflective progressions, use them for self-reflection and goal setting. The reflective progressions contain specific criteria useful when you are observing your own work. You may use them after viewing a video of yourself, or simply as a reflection upon completion of a training. Douglas Fisher and Nancy Frey (2012) suggest you focus on the idea of errors rather than on simple mistakes when considering and reviewing feedback. Be aware that correcting every single mistake is not only exhausting, but it may actually make you feel overwhelmed and frustrated. Rather, Fisher and Frey (2012) suggest, "Correcting mistakes while failing to address errors can be a costly waste of instructional time" (p. 42). What are the trends? What are consistent comments from many participants? How does what you read in the comments coincide with your own perception? With the progression as the basis of reflection, you are more likely to perceive feedback as constructive. Use this while reviewing a video of your presentation.

By using reflective progressions as the foundation for quality feedback and reflection, presenters can objectively identify strengths and challenges about their products or processes. The term for this is *metacognition*. It has been used to describe "knowing about one's own knowledge and knowledge about one's own performance" (Feltovich, Prietula, & Ericsson, 2006, p. 55). Self-reflection through metacognition is powerful.

As I mention previously in this chapter, be aware of the outliers. One overly positive or negative comment will happen. That's par for the course. One nasty, personalized comment from a disgruntled participant can shake you—seriously shake you. If there is brutal honesty that causes you to solidly reflect about that comment, by all means consider it. Yet, in all likelihood, your reflective survey was simply a chance for him or her to have a voice. Your survey instrument can sometimes be a passive-aggressive way for employees to share their thoughts with supervisors anonymously. It may have nothing to do with you. Also, some people simply strive to make others' lives miserable. Keep it in perspective. You are looking for consistent comments to create trends in performance. Maybe you received a dozen or more comments about your enthusiasm. Relish that. Make note. Repeat it. Or, maybe you received the same number of comments that stated your handout was difficult to follow. Look deeper into the comments of that trend for specific ways to improve your handout for next time. The worst thing you can do is nothing. If you are courageous enough to ask for feedback, then be equally courageous to use it to improve your practice.

A final thought about self-reflection is to understand that public speaking isn't for everyone. If your evaluation results, over time, continue to be more negative in nature and leave you feeling stressed, criticized, and incompetent, by all means, stop presenting for a while. Reassess your desire for this type of work. Some people have a natural propensity for public speaking. Others do not; rather, they work better sharing ideas more informally in small groups or even behind the scenes. It doesn't make you less of a professional. It might just be an opportunity for you to re-evaluate your reasons for becoming a professional speaker and if you do, indeed, want to continue on such a journey. Be honest with yourself. Even some of the most revered instructional coaches, principals, or district or state educational leaders may find migrating to professional speaking unnatural and frustrating. Professional speaking is extremely difficult, and it is not to be done by everyone or considered lightly.

Seeking Help From a Trusted Colleague

Another great resource in reflection is the use of a trusted colleague. It is important that the colleague you select have relevancy to presenting. In other words, someone who has never keynoted (or has not done so for many years) may not be as powerful a resource as someone who keynotes somewhat regularly. It doesn't mean that a nonpresenter cannot provide you with meaningful feedback. In fact, using the sample reflective progressions makes it easier for a nonpresenter to provide objective feedback. Yet, combining the reflective progressions from a seasoned presenter will be of highest value. This will likely make the reflection or conversation more productive and less personal.

These progressions provide an efficient set of criteria by which the trusted colleague denotes areas of success and challenge. If your focus is on the learning progression and not on the score, you will see colleague comments as helping you move along the learning progression of the scale. Making the reflective progression the centerpiece of the feedback discussion helps you see your colleagues' comments more objectively. Using reflective progressions as a basis for reflection is a great way to obtain more specific, quality feedback.

Using Quality Feedback for Goal Setting

Feedback comes in many forms using various methods, and may come before, during, or after you set your own goals. For instance, it may precede goal setting if you use the reflective progressions in the planning phases. Feedback may also occur during the learning journey, as the audience members provide feedback about their learning progress and understanding throughout the training. Feedback may also come after you have set initial goals and when you are reflecting about your progress toward goals based on specific feedback received from other sessions. Goal setting must be a more continuous process of learning how to learn.

Provide yourself time to reflect on your goals as an ongoing process. Begin by carving out time once to twice per week for reflection and goal setting. Plan and reflect about feedback obtained from trainings. These careful processes help you get better.

You may use figure 7.7 to consider the various components of feedback and self-reflection for the characteristics previously discussed.

This chart may assist you in using reflection feedback for goal setting. Note the major components for an effective presentation in the left-hand column. Refer to your reflective progression scores for each section. Where are your strengths? Challenges? What evidence do you have to support your thinking? Are there audience or host trends to support your comments? What goal (or goals) might you set? Such protocols can be helpful in reviewing your work and considering actionable goals.

Components for Effective Trainings	Audiences' and Hosts' Reflections	Likert Scale Results	My Reflection	My Goal Around This Component
Messaging (Content)				
Room Arrangement				
Introduction				
Audience Engagement				
Visual and Print Resources				
Conclusion				

Figure 7.7: Components of effective trainings.

*Visit **go.SolutionTree.com/leadership** for a free reproducible version of this figure.*

Summary

In this chapter, I focused on reflecting on how you delivered your message. How did it go? What is your evidence? Here I discussed the importance of reflection and feedback. Next, I explored what makes for solid presenter feedback. I provided suggestions for making your reflective surveys more useful and meaningful and including results with the goal-setting process. This will help you hone your craft for future trainings. The next chapter focuses on tips, tricks, and troubleshooting presentation situations.

Chapter 8

Presenting Tips, Tricks, and Troubleshooting

Being both soft and strong is a combination very few have mastered.

—Nona Gaya

As I've highlighted throughout this resource, presenting is tough. Nonetheless, perfecting your presentations is possible. In this chapter, I highlight a plethora of tips, tricks, and troubleshooting ideas to ease some of the gaffes inherent in this endeavor. I discuss how to best convey enthusiasm for your topic, how to avoid taking yourself seriously, and how to deal with poor behavior from audience members. Next, I describe how to model professionalism, introduce tips for handling question-and-answer sessions, and discuss considerations for traveling presenters.

Show Interest and Enthusiasm

Although showing interest and enthusiasm about the topic you are presenting seems simple enough, it is worth noting. When you care, your audience cares. In fact, there is some neuroscience research to support the idea that your enthusiasm with your topic is contagious to your audience. Early in the 1990s, researchers at University College London (officially known as UCL since 2005) and UCLA discovered mirror neurons. These mirror neurons are found mostly near the limbic system, which PBS (2007) details as follows:

> *Mirror neurons [are] a specific kind of brain cell that fires both when performing an action and when observing someone else perform the same action. It turns out that mirror neurons, which are normally associated with physical activities, might also be responsible for signaling the human brain's emotional system, which in turn allows us to empathize with other people.*

This quote exemplifies that mirror neurons actually help humans tap into others' emotions. Therefore, if you are interested in and enthusiastic about the topic you are presenting, it is more likely your audience will be, too. Exude enthusiasm through your verbal and nonverbal messages. Be certain your facial expressions match your voice intonation and interest. Don't overdo it, but be mindful of this. Sometimes, there is an awkward mismatch between intent and perception. As Michelle Obama (2018) states,

> *I went to David Axelrod's office in Chicago and sat down with him and Valerie to watch video of some of my public appearances. . . . But then Axe muted the volume as he replayed my stump speech, removing my voice so that we could look more closely at my body language, specifically my facial expressions. What did I see? I saw myself speaking with intensity and conviction and never letting up. . . . My face reflected the seriousness of what I believed was at stake. . . . But it was too serious, too severe—at least given what people were conditioned to expect from a woman. I saw my expression as a stranger might perceive it. . . . I could see now that there was a performative piece to politics that I hadn't yet fully mastered. . . . Bigger crowds required clearer facial cues, which was something I needed to work on. (pp. 267–268)*

What Obama realized is that perception is a reality and may not match intention. Therefore, be mindful of your perceived nonverbal behaviors. Do they match the message you want to convey? Is your interest and enthusiasm demonstrated without being misperceived as either overly passive or too assertive in nature?

Don't Take Yourself Too Seriously

You will make some inadvertent errors. You may slip up and invert letters while speaking; you may have a grammatical or spelling error on a presentation slide; you may physically trip. These are but a few examples of ways in which you will blunder. But do know, blunders will happen somewhere, sometime, and when you least expect it. I recall how I was organizing an audience to interact during a training session, and I meant to tell them to "find a partner." Unfortunately, the words that came out were "Pind a fartner." Yep. I said it, and aloud. At that moment, how you handle the situation will determine how your audience will, too. I acknowledged it. In fact, I asked, "Did I just say fartner?" The participants in the front row nodded and giggled. I covered my mouth, as to show my surprise; then I burst out laughing. It allowed the audience to do the same. Instead of trying to act like it didn't happen, I conceded, laughed at myself, and provided the entire group with a moment of levity. You are human. You will make mistakes. Own it, fix it, and don't repeat it. Your audience will take cues from you. If it is something you truly don't think is appropriate to repeat, don't do it. If you don't want to be sidetracked, just quickly admit the error and move on. Yet, share sincere moments of humanity. They help you relate to your audience. Participants will realize that you are no longer a talking head, coming to refute past efforts and make them change. Instead, you are mortal, just like them.

Address Poor Behaviors

Adults appreciate you setting up the parameters and behavioral expectations of one another. Yet, you will occasionally have audience members who violate such norms. In those instances, you must address it. This is the perfect time to introduce a continuum of interventions, not unlike those you might use with participants in a classroom. Figure 8.1 is a training version for consideration.

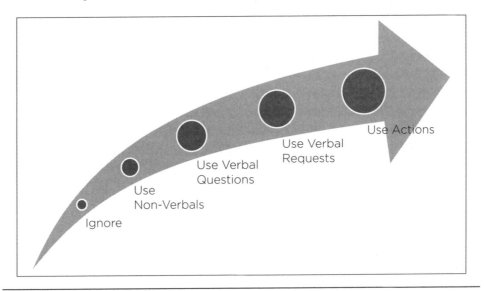

Figure 8.1: Progression for addressing misbehaviors.

Notice that the chart begins with ignoring and progresses through to more prominent actions. As you might assume, such presenter behaviors go from more covert to more overt in nature.

Choose to Ignore

Ignoring *is* a response to poor adult behavior, considering you actually are aware of the poor behavior. It is passive, yet it is a response. Essentially, you are electing to refrain from noting the behavior at that time and place and assuming it may get better later on. With adults, it often does. Sometimes, adults are aware they made a mistake, will avoid repeating it, and are happy to not be called out for a momentary infraction. However, note that ignoring is on the lower end of the intervention continuum and should only be used if the situation rectifies itself soon after.

Use Nonverbal Behaviors

From there, the continuum progresses to the use of nonverbal behaviors. Just like with participants in the grouproom, there are many options here. You may simply look over in the direction of the infraction. If that effectively halts the troublesome behavior, stop there. No more action is needed. If it doesn't, you will need to go further. Next, consider the almighty pause. Stop speaking for a few seconds. When the participants stop talking and return, thank them, smile, and move on.

If you are finding limited success with those nonverbal attempts, move to relative proximity—moving into the area of the off-task person or table group. If your presence in the vicinity doesn't modify the adult behaviors, move closer. In fact, move very close to—almost hovering over—the main perpetrator. It will feel uncomfortable. It is intended to. This sends a clear message that you are aware of the infractions and you are attempting to remedy the situation. Then, wait a bit. Provide time for the behaviors to change. In fact, present your next small section from that location. (Note: do you recall again why it is so important for you to know your content so well?) Now, wait again. Combine catching the eye of the culprits along with your use of proximity. As you do, discern whether the misbehavior (often talking) is relevant to the task at hand. If it is, be a bit more tolerant with adult learners. Educators, by nature, are verbal processors. This might also be a signal to you that they need a table team discussion or you need to provide more opportunities for their reflection and reaction. If not, you will need to take more obtrusive action.

As with all of these suggestions, if your response stops the misbehavior, mission accomplished. There is no need to take it any further. However, if it doesn't, progress up the continuum with different uses of nonverbals. You might try pointing to something you are asking the group to reference. If appropriate, you may even elect to try the universal "sh" signal. By this time, everyone in your audience is aware of the infraction and the fact that you are working to address it. Don't underestimate that last part of that phrase. Audiences, like participants in a grouproom, want you to address poor behaviors. There is little worse than setting up expectations and not enforcing them. Neglecting to enforce expectations will instantly hurt your credibility with the entire group. In fact, remember that often these misbehaviors are not unique to you or this training. Adults who intentionally misbehave have been allowed to do so before. You will find out later (in evaluation comments) that adult audience members appreciate you working to address training issues. They really do.

Use Verbal Behaviors

One way to start verbally addressing the behaviors is simply to go back and use your attention signal with the verbal attention refocus cue. If the noise is remaining and the time for redirection is getting uncomfortably long, you may add, "If you can see my signal and hear my voice, please help those around you." This phrase works well. Once you have the group refocused, thank the participants for rejoining and respecting your attention signal. Another idea is to address the inattentive group by a table number. You may even say something like, "Table 12, please rejoin us. Thanks." This, of course, only works if you have assigned table numbers previously.

If you find yourself still achieving limited results with the off-task behaviors, take a formal break. However, during that break, have a private conversation with the main offenders. Say something like "I realize that I am not meeting your needs during the training right now. What can I do better?" Taking this approach puts the onus on you, and will cause the adult (or adults) involved to be more receptive and less offended toward you and your comments. Often, such participants will admit to their off-task behaviors, and you can thank them for recognizing it. Then, address the norms in question: "Thanks for your help in coming back together when asked to do so. It really helps us keep our focus and stay on time." Thank them again for any attempt to own the behavior and work toward fixing it. Then, kindly smile at them throughout the next sections of your presentation and even thank them privately.

Use Verbal Behaviors With Spin and Walk Away

You have tried a myriad of nonverbal and professionally stated verbal responses to no avail. If you now get the "Who, me?!" response after your verbal request, then simply describe (in some detail) the behavior the group members are doing and ask them to kindly change it. It might sound something like "When I'm speaking to the group, your team is using normal voices to talk during the presentation, and that is distracting to others. Please refrain from talking when others are speaking. Thanks." As the conversation ends, use what I call the *spin and walk away*. This means that you deliver the verbal description of the behavior (carefully refraining from a judgment statement) in a manner that simply describes what you are noticing and what you would like to see participants do instead. Afterward, listen for any respectful response, then remove yourself from any potential argument or defensiveness by physically spinning on the balls of your feet and walking away. You may need to practice this strategy if it is new to you. Stand up. Lean in and say a kind, professional, memorized phrase like "Please respond to our attention signal more consistently." Then, smile (not sarcastically!), spin on the balls of both feet, and walk at least seven to ten steps away. This gets you out of earshot and away from the situation for a bit. It also sends a direct message that you are done and not interested in arguing or discussing it more at that time. It is a powerful strategy that keeps you from getting too emotionally involved, and provides those involved time to adjust.

Use Verbal Behaviors First, Break Second

You may elect to give the misbehaving person or group time away during the break first, and address the participants later as they return. Yet, I advise addressing the situation *before* they leave the room. The reasons are twofold. First, you will catch them as there begins some commotion in the room as people are getting up, moving, and talking, so as to provide you with background noise as privacy. Second, it provides a small amount of time for the perpetrators to think about what you said, maybe even discuss it out of your hearing range, and make the necessary modifications. That small amount of time can also work as a cooling-off period so they can reflect and correct. It comes back to the emotional brain reasoning discussed previously (Feinstein, 2006). The initial conversation may incur an emotional response on both your part and theirs. A bit of time can actually mitigate the emotion. As the person or group returns, be kind. Be professional. Acknowledge your appreciation in a smile and seek ways to draw the person or small group into your presentation in a positive manner. Be sure you know and use the participants' names, as you recall from chapter 4 (page 37).

Use Verbal Behaviors by Revisiting Norms

As groups settle back after break, repost and revisit the group norms you established at the onset of the day. Doing so re-establishes your expectations and helps the group members monitor their own behaviors. In fact, sometimes, after a break or lunch, you may use the strategy of asking all participants to reflect on a norm they may need to monitor a bit more during the second half of the training. Give them time to read the norms and a bit of time for silent reflection. I would refrain from having them discuss this. Simply move forward, and thank them, in advance, for adhering to the norms.

Use or modify the group roles previously established. Do you need someone to monitor norms? If so, seek help from each table in doing so. Maybe you add that to an existing role, like the facilitator. You are basically giving individuals the authority to monitor their group's behaviors toward the established norms. Although it might ultimately be limited in actual application, it sends a message that those are behaviors to which all participants need to attend. It might also put your audience members back on their best behavior.

Now may also be the time to recognize participant realities. For example, maybe you just found out that participants had parent-teacher conferences until late into the evening the night before. Recognize them for what they might be feeling, and offer them a few additional breaks, a bit more time during discussions, or even the option to forgo the last break and get out fifteen minutes early (as long as you cleared that with your host!). The key here is empathy. Remember that listening isn't easy. Learning can be strenuous, and learning about a difficult topic can be even more difficult. A little empathy goes a long way in helping your audience members recognize their needs to be human, too. You might even make a deal, saying something like "I realize this is a bit difficult, yet if you can give me thirty more minutes, I'll build in a reflection and application time." There, again, is the need for your flexibility and your preplanned activity options. It may also be a chance for you to locate a lighthearted video or a motivating quote with which to end. Do your very best to leave your audiences, even somewhat disrespectful ones, inspired.

Take Action

In extremely rare instances, you may need to combine the previously mentioned strategies with a more intensive action.

Find Out More

If you recognize that a participant is being not only inattentive but also disrespectful to you and others, discuss this with your host. Is there something you need to know? Did the participant just receive tragic news and thus is he or she simply tolerating the session as part of a contractual agreement? You never know someone's story. I remember once being quite frustrated at a principal's behavior with his team. He was talking (loudly) during the direct instruction time, almost incessantly. I tried many of the aforementioned strategies, only to discover during my conversation with him at break that he was all but deaf in one ear, and was constantly checking with others to clarify his understanding about what I was saying. Again, you never know someone's story, and to assume that you do is dangerous. Although I was put off during the first portion of that initial training, I had a renewed appreciation for his needs. We planned together ways in which I would speak closer to his table so he could read my lips. I would also slow down a bit, and provide more small-group discussions so he could check his understanding. Understanding his situation made all the difference.

Use the Sticky Note Strategy

One of my colleagues, and coauthor, uses a sticky note strategy quite effectively. This involves writing a requested action on a sticky note and placing it at the seat of the offender (or table of offenders) during break. The sticky note might read, "Please monitor your use of your technology. Thanks!" Then, sign your name. This makes it personal, yet not confrontational. After using this strategy one time, members of the small group I addressed came up at the end of the first day of the two-day session, apologized for their misbehavior, and promised to change it for the next day. It was a respectful redirection on my part, and an equally respectful admission and remediation of the situation on theirs. I believe we all achieved an even higher respect for one another that would not have happened had I elected to ignore the behavior.

Elicit Help

Sometimes, you have exhausted your resources. By this time, many in the room are aware of your countless attempts to redirect the behavior, all the while maintaining your professionalism. In fact, expect some of them to apologize for the wrongdoer (or wrong-doers). This happens so often. Yet, the show must go on. Does your host have insights in dealing with that individual or group thereof? Seek ideas from others in charge of the training. Consider one of these five options: (1) the misbehavior might mean that a supervisor needs to be seated at the table; (2) the seating arrangement may necessitate modifications; (3) the host may need to intervene with the person or persons individually; (4) the person or group's supervisor needs to be informed at the conclusion of the training; or, ultimately, (5) the person or persons may need to be removed from the audience. Do this as a last resort. Just try to keep adult misbehaviors from becoming so personalized that you are paralyzed. The rest of the group needs you. You have a job to do. Find your inner peace, and press on with the utmost professionalism.

Apologize

Most misbehaviors aren't personal. In fact, some people don't even realize the effect of their actions. Yet, some participant misbehaviors *are* intended to push you. Some participants will actually do so in order to achieve a small sense of power in a seemingly powerless situation for them. Others will challenge you in order to see what you know and if your experiences earn their respect. Your responsiveness to the situation is important. Remember, it's just behavior, which is a manifestation of deeper needs on the part of an audience member.

After an atypical behavioral situation occurs, I always reflect and ask myself if I would do anything differently. A very few times, the answer is yes. Most times, it's no. When you take the high road, you can't go wrong. However, if there is a time you let your emotions take over, remember the saying—admit it, fix it, and don't repeat it. Admit it to the person you may have inadvertently offended or wronged. It can happen, even after you take precautions not to do so. If you messed up, own it. Be sincere. Apologize for it. Don't make an excuse, as that will negate the sincerity of the apology. During the apology, seek ways to make it right. Do you need to follow up with someone personally, via email, or with a personal phone call? Express your learning from the situation and your commitment to never repeating it. Again, we are all humans in a very important, yet humanly interactive situation. Above all, be professional even in the midst of unprofessional behaviors.

Model Professionalism

Exude verbal and nonverbal behaviors you would expect of the utmost professional. Speak about what you know about, and tread lightly around those things you don't. Keep your voice neutral during more heated conversations or situations, and work so others cannot easily read any negative emotions—even when they are brewing inside. You might need to practice this neutral face by looking in a mirror while imagining an incident that evoked some negative emotion. Notice how you look. What is your posture? Is your brow furrowed? Could anyone tell how irked you are? Some emotion is natural—you don't want to look like a paralyzed, expressionless statue. Yet, an overly emotional presenter triggers stress within the audience members.

Professionalism means you speak kindness to your group, even if some jabs come your way. As Valorie Burton (2016) says,

> If the person with whom you are conversing is foolish, speaking nonsense, and attempting to engage you in conversation that will require you to stoop down to a level of ignorance, do not engage. Ease out of the conversation, decline to comment, or walk away. Anything you attempt to say in such a situation will likely only escalate the conversation. (p. 147)

It's fine to have and use an assertive tone to make a point or calmly dispute a heckler, but never allow it to move into frustration or anger. You'll come off like a tantrum-throwing toddler. Use strategies to deflect apparent verbal throw-down traps. One I like is called *critical issues*. I simply write that title on a large piece of chart paper, and I add the concern or issue (quoted by the individual, as best I can, as it emulates his or her voice and topic, not yours) to the chart paper. This allows you to honor it, yet place it elsewhere for later and further discussion. It stops an argument and allows you to get back on track. This strategy is great to use when someone raises an irrelevant issue or an emotional one, and you want to note it but not deal with it at that time. I keep the same chart paper up throughout the training. Time permitting, I will either address the issue(s) right after lunch or a break, as a quick transition. Or, I may ask the person with the critical issue to see me during a break or at the conclusion of the training to offer information about a topic that is important, yet not pertinent to the entire group. Sometimes, it is an issue about which needs attention from the school or district team.

Monitor your use of your personal devices. Only use them when you would desire your audience to do so—at breaks, during lunch, and at the conclusion of the session. Not only can these devices be a mental distraction for you, but using them outwardly sends a message that the training at hand is not important. It's subtle, yet remember you are always being observed—even during breaks.

During breaks and lunch, refrain from any gossip or judgment about others. Often you will observe the dynamics of those around you, and you may need to change topics or refocus the discussion. Also, refrain from speaking to a co-trainer or colleague about anyone or thing that occurred during the session or training day until you are *out* of the parking lot, and completely away from the presentation location. Of course, if you need to address something with an attendee or host, please do so. You simply never want a comment to be heard or misinterpreted by unknowing listeners as you exit the location. It's always amazing how many people overhear things in hallways, in bathrooms, or near the cars in the parking lot. Never—ever—speak negatively about anyone within earshot of others. It says more about you than the person who is referenced. Save your own need to "vent" until you are with a trusted partner or friend, but nowhere near the site. Simply practice professionalism and tactfulness.

Handle Question-and-Answer Sessions Appropriately

Question-and-answer sessions help personalize a training situation. They can also be the worst of detractors and an emotional gorge. If you use this format at some point in your session, be sure *you* set it up and manage it. As I wrote in chapter 4, inform your audience how you intend to seek and respond to questions. Determine your own preference for an allotted time frame or whether you will accept questions peppered throughout. The choice is yours. Yet, be certain that you manage questions in a way to keep the focus on the topic at hand and ensure that you will maintain your command of the room and authority of the topic. A few suggestions for effective Q&A include the following.

- **Repeat the question asked:** Better yet, have the questioner ask it into a microphone. That way his or her voice is connected with it, not yours. It also allows you a bit more time to craft a thoughtful response, and it ensures that everyone heard the question. Clarify with the questioner that you heard it and understood it as it was intended.

- **Maintain eye contact with the questioner while he or she is asking the question, and on and off as you complete your answer to it:** It personalizes your response, yet allows you to pan the room throughout the response, so as to bring others from the audience into the discussion.

- **If you sense irritation or frustration in the voice of a questioner, give him or her your full attention and listen respectfully:** Don't interrupt. If you deem it is a negative comment rather than a question, ask the person to clarify or give an example of his or her concern. This makes the questioner think deeply about what is being said and doesn't allow for a random "Yeah, but . . ." kind of ploy. If you need to, simply acknowledge this concern, and respond respectfully with something like "That is one consideration I've not noticed or seen, yet a concern to be surfaced, nonetheless." Then, move on.

- **If you see hands pop up with fervor while you are speaking, let the questioner know you see his or her hand, yet finish your thought or statement before calling upon him or her:** Finish your sentence and nod or acknowledge the hand, but don't allow it to interrupt your thought or your spoken phrase. Allow the question as you have completed your phrase. It keeps you in control of the room.

- **If you don't know an answer to a question, say so:** Thank the person for asking, and simply reply that you don't know at this time. I like to then follow up with the option for the questioner to send me an email with the question. This strategy allows you time to seek the answer and places the responsibility for pursuing an answer back to the questioner. If it's real, he or she will email you. If it's not, he or she won't bother.

Providing your participants time to seek more information about their questions customizes your training topic. Do so with thoughtfulness, with professionalism, and within a reasonable time frame.

Make Travel Arrangements That Make Sense

Travel arrangements add another layer of stress to an already stressful public speaking venture. Here I will detail a few travel tips to keep you from losing your mind.

Book Early and Travel Respectfully

Book hotels and flights as soon as possible—within twenty days for the better deals, and on Tuesday or Wednesday. Booking them together through some online booking agencies may be beneficial. If you begin to travel more frequently away from your home location, you'll need to decide which airlines and hotels are your preference and meet your budget. Pay close attention to those airlines with the most direct flights, as this will save you agony with fewer delayed flights and tight connections. Immediately sign up for their rewards programs, and be patient for the rewards to materialize. You will often have to fly thousands of miles and over dozens of segments to get enough credit to obtain any type of status. Once you do gain it, avoid the pressure to act entitled or snobbish.

Ensure you know how to board and disembark a plane respectfully. Avoid jumping ahead in line (unless you are in an urgent situation—then pay it forward, later). Pack a carry-on bag that is actually a carry-on size. Regular travelers become easily annoyed by those who still think their fifty-pound monstrous suitcase will fit if they push, prod, and shove it long enough. It won't. So, please stop trying! Get a good set of noise-canceling headphones. They come in handy with crying babies (who can't help it), and, not to mention, they will allow you uninterrupted time to focus on your presentation (or yourself!) away from chatty fellow passengers.

Maximize Your Time

Your plane rides will now become your mini-office space. Plan accordingly. That means using this time to fine-tune and personalize your presentations. That concentrated hour or two can really be useful. Take your needed resources, review your presentation and handout, add page numbers to your slides, and otherwise take this time to perfect your presentation.

A word of caution: don't rely on using the internet. Airline internet access is expensive and unreliable. Most airports have decent connections, yet most aren't secure. Consider using a personal hotspot. It will come in handy not only in airports, but also in training venues with locked internet.

Use Apps for Efficiency

There are oodles of apps to make travel more manageable. By the time this goes to print, I'm sure a hundred more will be available and applicable. A few I appreciate are listed in table 8.1 (page 84).

Table 8.1: Apps for Making Travel More Efficient

Applications	Brief Description
Airline apps	They allow for automated check-in, notifications, and boarding passes.
Sleep Cycle	This serves as a soothing alarm, as well as a tracker for when best to wake you during an REM sleep cycle.
Wallet	This Apple app collates all boarding passes from any airline.
Key Ring	This app keeps all the previous loyalty cards and corresponding numbers at your fingertips. So, when you need rewards numbers, they are all in one place.
Travel itinerary apps (TripIt, Concur)	These apps collect and organize all of your travel parts into one comprehensive itinerary.
Hotel rewards apps	These are for respective hotels and allow for electronic check-in, special requests, and electronic keys that allow you to bypass the desk upon arrival.
Rental car apps	These apps also allow for electronic check-in, car preferences, and perks.
SeatGuru	This app helps you see the best type of seat for the model and type of plane you are flying on, as well as if there are electrical outlets. It is especially helpful for long and overseas flights.
FlightView	This is one of many apps that allow you to track flights by flight number, location of origin, and expected arrival location.
Navigation apps like Google Maps, Apple Maps, and Waze	These essential apps provide step-by-step directions, maps, and verbal prompts for you while driving in unknown locations.
Uber, Lyft	These apps allow you to bypass the rental car services and use a car service. Be certain your location has one prior to making plans. Some remote locations do not.
Your favorite restaurant apps	These allow you to preorder food and have delivery or pickup options for ease in eating better foods while on the road.
Health apps like Simply Yoga, Mindbody, Beachbody, MyFitnessPal, 7-Minute Workout, Runtastic Road Bike, Calm, Runkeeper, Headspace, or Meditation	These help you work out, meditate, and practice mindfulness while on the road.

As you might imagine, the apps are limitless and readily available. Think about what you are accustomed to doing at home, and consider getting apps to assist you in maintaining that type of connection and normalcy while traveling. You will need supports, as travel is grueling.

Take Care of Yourself

Plan ahead to eat well, sleep as best you can, practice positive self-talk, and keep physically fit. Eating on the road is really, really challenging. Even if you make wise choices (the carrots instead of the chips), you won't often be able to control how your food is prepared. Even something as simple as ordering decaffeinated coffee may end up haunting you at 3:00 a.m., when you realize the server didn't remember decaf or didn't want to make a fresh pot of it!

Sleeping away from home is difficult for most, although I see some people who can fall asleep during the loudest flight or even with unruly hotel neighbors. Those walls are paper thin, so plan for it. A set of earplugs will be well worth it when you realize the college basketball team is roomed right next door, or the guest above you walks like an elephant at odd times during the night. Needless to say, sleeping in hotels is not always fun, nor is it always easy. Plan to become a bit sleep deprived the first night at least. Your natural fight-or-flight system may cause you to hear every sound—each siren, passing semitrailer, and garbage truck. If you count on a good night's sleep the first night in a hotel, expect to be disappointed.

Expect the Unexpected

Find ways to calm yourself with positive self-talk. You'll need it when your flight is delayed and you miss the connecting one, or when the passenger near you takes all the space and wants to talk the entire flight, or maybe when the rental car company has no cars left at 1:00 a.m., even though you have a confirmed reservation. Whatever happens, you will need to put a smile on your face and talk yourself through it. Things will happen, people will irritate you, and situations will be out of your control. How you respond will either cause you more stress or allow you to help limit the stress and even defuse potentially volatile situations. In the end, it's your response to the situation that will either drive you crazy or make you laugh and write a book about the "You won't believe this one" moments.

Pack medicines and remedies for unexpected illnesses. Have something available for intestinal issues, as travel will make you more susceptible to indigestion, food poisoning, and the stomach flu. Pack supplies for the common cold, headaches, muscle aches, and the multitude of other potential ailments. Also, ensure you have some powder electrolyte packets, as you can easily add them to water for severe dehydration that occurs often and can be easily overlooked. Dehydration can pose disastrous results. In fact, hydrate every chance you get while flying. You must be conscious of it, and plan for it.

There is little worse than being ill thousands of miles from home, maybe even in a different country, in a hotel room with no one to help you. I've had to deal with many situations. My least favorite was having the stomach flu during the fifteen-hour flight to Australia. Truly, I don't think I've endured much worse (and I gave birth without any pain medications!). Yet, hotel staff are kind and helpful. Ask for help when you need it. They make chicken soup and will run and get you sports drinks at all hours of the morning or night, if you request politely.

Pack Purposefully

If you find yourself working a great deal from home, packing may become your nemesis. It is one of my least favorite things to do! Be certain you look ahead at the weather forecast of where you will be heading—especially if it is a drastically different climate from where you live. Forgetting a heavy coat and gloves while in Minnesota in January will either require you to expend money you hadn't anticipated or cause you to be extremely uncomfortable. I begin by packing around my shoes. They are my most important outfit accompaniment, and if I'm gone for multiple days, I have a color theme in order for accessories to be multipurpose. While packing, I learned a trick to keep me from ironing. (Anything that keeps me from this awful task is worth noting!) First, invest in clothing that is wrinkle free and travel friendly. Then, as you pack, layer every fold of your clothing in between plastic dry-cleaner bags or tissue paper. This keeps them from sliding and limits wrinkles. It works! I haven't ironed clothes while on the road for many years. Carry within your supplies some wrinkle releaser spray. As you unpack in your hotel room, spray, hang, and wear.

If you use multiple suitcases for various lengths of trips, then stash a complete set of necessary toiletries in every different bag. This way, you can easily unpack and repack, without transferring items you will certainly want and need for the next trip. Remember to include special items that bring you comfort in sterile hotel rooms. For instance, I love to include an electric toothbrush and various aromatic scents to help me relax. If you do this long enough, you will relish the small luxuries of home—soft towels, cushioned bathroom mats, and plush bedding.

Invest in suitcases that are durable and functional. I prefer hard-sided, four-wheeled versions. I even have a favorite brand. You don't have to spend a fortune on good suitcases, but be sure what you purchase will fit the dimensions you need and have the functionality you demand. Use work satchel roller bags, as they will save your back, shoulders, and neck. Backpacks with handle sleeves for slipping over your roller carry-on are great, too.

Summary

A few tips, tricks of the trade, and troubleshooting ideas can be the best advice you receive. In this chapter, I detailed suggestions for showing genuine interest and enthusiasm for your topic, laughing at your inadvertent mistakes, and handling participant misbehaviors, as well as travel suggestions and hacks. Experience is a great trainer or facilitator in the professional speaking world. Learn from each success and mistake, store it away, and use it as needed. The next section of this resource shares a plethora of processes and protocols you can infuse and use throughout your various speaking engagements.

PART 2   Processes and Protocols

Processes and protocols are key for making professional development interactive. In fact, the more of them you include in your repertoire, the more agile you will be as a presenter. Thoughtful and intentional use of processes and protocols is often the difference between a mediocre facilitated session or training and a great one.

One word of caution is to use them purposefully. Be certain you consider the group size guidelines, as space and materials may impede effectiveness. Be mindful of *clearly* describing and modeling (when appropriate) the protocol. I advise you to provide written directions in addition to verbal ones. You may also use a demonstration group to model the process or protocol to increase the success of its use. Carefully match the protocol to your group. Some groups may be more playful and may tolerate a more gamelike structure. Others may deem the activity childish. At any rate, make the decision to use it, and *make* it effective. In other words, own it. If you seem uncertain about its use, your group will too. Try new protocols with smaller groups first, so as to work out any potential kinks in setting them up or using them effectively. Then, add your own variations. Enjoy! These can be fun.

The remaining chapters are filled with a variety of processes and protocols for you to reference. For each, you will see the title, the purpose, the time frame and logistics, the description of it, and any variations for consideration. For ease in referencing, the processes and protocols are organized in chapters according to their primary purpose. Knowing why you want a group to interact is paramount. The purposes include:

- Team building (chapter 9, page 89)

- Triggering thinking (chapter 10, page 109)

- Processing or practicing (chapter 11, page 117)

- Consensus building (chapter 12, page 137)

- Summarizing (chapter 13, page 141)

- Checking for understanding (chapter 14, page 155)

Helpful online resources and software programs are listed for your convenience in the appendix (page 163).

Although the purpose for each process or protocol is specified, others may be reasonable. For example, a team-building activity may also serve for triggering thinking about a topic. Within each chapter, the protocols are then alphabetized.

These processes and protocols are a conglomeration of various great minds. Many are variations from Kagan (1994), Lipton and Wellman (2016), and the School Reform Initiative (n.d.b), who previously and thoughtfully crafted strategies for grouping participants in cooperative ways. Others have been shared by colleagues, and still others have been crafted while in the midst of training situations. Because adaptations to the following processes and protocols are endless, I offer general recognition and thanks to the many great minds before us.

Chapter 9

Team Building

In this chapter, you will find twenty-six presentation strategies that focus on *team building*. You may choose to use team-building strategies when you are working with new groups, after breaks for a quick transition and fun experience, or when you are facilitating a session. These activities will help your audience engage with one another, learn more about one another, and build the trust among team members that may be necessary for activities you conduct later in your presentation.

Within each strategy, you will find a brief introduction that explains its concept and purpose, a description of the time the activity takes and the materials needed, and a series of steps for implementing the strategy. On occasion, the strategy may also include a couple of variations you may choose to implement, depending on what you wish to achieve with the strategy, the makeup of your group, or the materials available.

Candy Matching

The Candy Matching strategy is a quick way to get members of a team talking and interacting as they debate which piece of candy matches the questions you ask them to share about themselves. This simple activity helps establish an environment of discussion and collaboration, which can aid in later activities that require teamwork and team discussion.

Time: 20 minutes

Materials: A basket of candy, string, scissors, and a ruler

Description: Use the following steps to implement the Candy Matching strategy.

1. Write a clue on paper and have the group individually or in teams attempt to match up the clue with a candy name. For examples, see figure 9.1.

Clue	Answer
Famous baseball player	Babe Ruth
Male name	Oh Henry
Bumpy street	Rocky Road
Our galaxy	Milky Way
Funny laugh	Snickers
Happy nut	Almond Joy

Figure 9.1: Example clues and answers for the Candy Matching strategy.

2. Have individuals or teams share out their responses.

Variations:

- This variation allows participants to reveal truths about themselves, instead of answers to a clue. Instruct participants to choose four candies from the bowl without looking. Once everyone has selected their candies, reveal a key code indicating which truths the participants should tell.

   Key code example: Kit Kat = favorite movie, favorite magazine, favorite song, or favorite book; Krackel = favorite vacation spot, place you would like to visit, place you would least like to visit, or worst vacation; lollipop = number of years in current position, where you work, what you do, or brief description of first job; gum drop = something about where you live, something about where you grew up, something about your family, or something about your town/city; Hershey's Kiss = wildcard (tell us anything).

- Instead of using a key code, allow people to take as many candies as they like from the basket and reveal something random about themselves for each candy they take.

- Use a ball of string. Allow people to take as much string as they like. For each inch, they must reveal something about themselves.

Card Grouping

The Card Grouping strategy is a way to mix up group members, allowing them to interact with others, as they use playing cards to group and regroup. This simple activity helps establish an environment of discussion and collaboration, which can aid in later activities that require teamwork and team discussion.

Time: 5–15 minutes

Materials: A deck of playing cards or multiple card decks. Be certain you have a large enough group to mix cards thoroughly. Otherwise, you may need to take out certain numbers or amounts of cards to ensure your group can mix by variations.

Description: Use the following steps to implement the Card Grouping strategy.

1. Begin by having each participant take one playing card.

2. Call out the type of grouping you want. For example, "Please group with one other person who has the same color of card as you." Continue to group participants by suit, color, pairs, runs, and so on.

3. Ask participants to begin discussion by sharing something about themselves (a simple introduction).

4. Consider then having these new teams discuss the content for a practicing idea.

Variations:

- Use cards to identify table groups (or even individuals) for sharing information. For example, you might say, "I'd like to hear from a table that has a red suit." This identification would occur after a table group has the opportunity to discuss something related to the content.

- Use the cards to mix and modify groups. For instance, you might say, "Please move into a group with two pairs of the same card represented."

Colored Candies

The Colored Candies strategy is a way for participants to find out information about one another.

Time: 10–15 minutes

Materials: Colored candies (for example, M&M's, Skittles, and so on)

Description: Use the following steps to implement the Colored Candies strategy.

1. Pass around a bag of colored candies.

2. Have participants take as many as they want.

3. For each color of candy, prepare a question they can answer. For instance, red can be "Name your favorite movie."

Variations:

- Consider using other colored objects rather than candies (paper clips, plastic figures, and so on).

- Consider creating wild card or bonus questions if participants take two or more candies of the same color.

Compass Points

The Compass Points activity's purpose is to help participants understand their own and others' behavior preferences. It is a great activity to help leadership teams or PLC teams understand learning and processing preferences in order to better understand their colleagues.

Time: 15–30 minutes

Materials: Four signs displaying the words indicated in the description, sticky tape for hanging signs

Description: Use the following steps to implement the Compass Points strategy.

1. Place signs containing the following descriptions for each direction around the room, or display them on a visual slide for reflection.

   a. **North:** *Acting—"Let's do it"; likes to act, try things, plunge in*

   b. **South:** *Caring—likes to know that everyone's feelings have been taken into consideration and that everyone's voices have been heard before acting*

   c. **East:** *Speculating—likes to look at the big picture and the possibilities before acting*

   d. **West:** *Paying attention to detail—likes to know the who, what, when, where, and why before acting*

   Note: You may want to reference the various descriptions of the directions during the discussion. Print out either the descriptions or the reflective questions to allow for this.

2. Invite participants to go to the direction of their choice. Instruct participants that no one will feel wholly represented by only one direction, but everyone can choose a predominant one.

3. Instruct each direction group to answer the following five questions:

   a. What are the strengths of your style? (four adjectives)

   b. What are the limitations of your style? (four adjectives)

   c. Which style do you find most difficult to work with, and why?

   d. What do people from the other directions or styles need to know about you so you can work together effectively?

   e. What do you value about the other three styles?

Variations:

- Note the distribution of participants among the directions. What might it mean?

- Discuss what is the best combination for a group to have. Does it matter?

- Discuss how you can avoid being driven crazy by another direction.

Descriptor Bingo

Descriptor Bingo is an interactive strategy for members to learn about others in the room. You may elect to complete the activity all at once, or reference it throughout the session by starting with one Bingo, then coming back for two Bingos, then going to blackout (finding someone for every square).

Time: 5–15 minutes

Materials: Previously prepared Bingo sheets relating to the typical characteristics of the group, pens or pencils

Description: Use the following steps to implement the Descriptor Bingo strategy.

1. Begin with a Bingo sheet that has descriptions you might note among a group of adults (for example, is over six feet tall, has dark hair, or was born in the sixties).

2. Participants mingle, finding others in the room with the listed characteristics, until they obtain a Bingo.

Variations:

- Modify the Bingo sheets with blackouts and diagonal requirements.

- Complete only one Bingo line prior to morning break. After lunch, repeat with the requirement to get two Bingos before completing the task.

- Add additional requirements to the Bingo sheet (for example, participants may not use one person for more than one Bingo cell).

Famous Person Mystery

This strategy helps participants interact with one another.

Time: 10–12 minutes

Materials: Sticky notes with the names of famous people

Description: Use the following steps to implement the Famous Person Mystery strategy.

1. The name of a famous person, living or deceased, is written on sticky notes.

2. The facilitator places one sticky note on the back of each participant.

3. Without looking, participants try to guess the name of the person on their back by asking questions that require only yes or no answers. For instance, "Am I alive or dead?" "Am I male?"

Variations:

- Instead of famous people, use famous landmarks, objects, or other categories.

- Use participants' famous people identities throughout your presentation to group the participants in different ways or select someone to respond.

- Consider three additional characteristics of the famous people identified in the first round.

"Find Someone Who..." Bingo

"Find Someone Who . . ." Bingo is a tried and true strategy that encourages participants to seek out others in the large group who have answers to specific questions describing themselves.

Time: 10 minutes

Materials: Premade "Find Someone Who . . ." questionnaire sheet, writing instrument

Description: Use the following steps to implement the "Find Someone Who . . ." Bingo strategy.

1. The presenter creates a blank Bingo card and fills in each square with questions or statements. For example, you might ask who

has a rescue pet, who likes sparkling water, who has paraglided, and the like.

2. Participants walk around the room seeking others who match with one of the questions.

3. The activity continues until someone obtains a Bingo.

Variations:

- Play *blackout*, where everyone has to find someone for each square represented.

- Require the group to complete a diagonal Bingo.

Finish the Sentence

Finish the Sentence gets members of a team talking and interacting as they learn about one another. This simple activity helps establish an environment of discussion and collaboration, which can aid in later activities that require teamwork and team discussion.

Time: 10–15 minutes

Materials: Premade question cards (or questions to be displayed on a screen or chart paper)

Description: Use the following steps to implement the Finish the Sentence strategy.

1. Go around the room and have participants complete one of these sentences (or something similar):

   a. The best job I ever had was . . .

   b. The worst project I ever worked on was . . .

   c. The riskiest thing I have ever done was . . .

2. This is a good technique for moving on to a new topic or subject. For example, when you are starting a class and you want learners to introduce themselves, you can have them complete the sentence, "I am in this class because . . ."

3. You can also move on to a new subject by asking a leading question. For example, if you are instructing time management, ask the leading question, "The one time I felt most stressed because I did not have enough time was . . ."

Variations:

- Record sentence prompts to be used in this activity on strips of paper, and place them in an envelope in the center of the table. Each participant chooses one strip of paper. One participant reads the sentence prompt, and everyone takes thirty to sixty seconds to complete the prompt. At the end of the "think time," each participant shares a response. The next person then shares the prompt on his or her piece of paper (and so on).

- Have participants write prompt questions for each other, and place them in a bowl in the center of the table. Then, have each participant draw and answer a prompt.

Life Boxes

Life Boxes is a quick way to get members of a team talking and interacting as they learn more about one another.

Time: 15 minutes

Materials: Paper and colored pencils, crayons or markers

Description: Use the following steps to implement the Life Boxes strategy.

1. Have participants take a sheet of paper and fold it in half, and then in half again.

2. Instruct participants to unfold the paper so they have four boxes.

3. Provide markers or crayons, and have participants write the following headings in the four boxes: (1) Childhood, (2) High School, (3) College, and (4) Future.

4. In each of the boxes, have participants draw a simple picture that represents an event or action that was extremely important to that particular time of their life.

5. Have people go around and share their experiences.

Name Chain

In Name Chain, members of a team share information about themselves. The activity encourages fun responses for impromptu ideas.

Time: 10–15 minutes

Materials: None

Description: Use the following steps to implement the Name Chain strategy.

1. The facilitator starts by sharing an object or entity (such as an adjective, a fruit, an animal, or a superhero) somewhat associated with themselves, and then says his or her name.

2. The next person says the facilitator's name and chosen adjective, fruit, animal, or superhero, then states his or her name and gives an additional adjective, fruit, animal, or superhero related to him or her.

3. Repeat around a team or group.

Variations:

- Have participants complete the prompt, "My name is _____, and I _____." Each person repeats the previous one's name and characteristic, and adds to the sentence by sharing about him- or herself. (For example, I say, "My name is Susan, and I like to golf." The next person says, "Her name is Susan, and she likes to golf. My name is Aaron, and I am from Texas.")

- Consider adding requirements to the characteristic (for example, by requiring that the person's name and characteristic must both start with the same letter).

On All Sides

This activity can be used to help teams connect or reconnect by learning more about one another.

Time: 10–12 minutes

Materials: Questions about personal characteristics for partners to address

Description: Use the following steps to implement the On All Sides strategy.

1. Assemble the group in a large open area.

2. Tell the participants that you'll call out for them to "find a partner."

3. Once they have a partner, call out either "side by side," "back to back," or "face to face." Partners should arrange themselves accordingly.

4. For side by side, partners should share vital statistics (for example, name, age, or hometown). For back to back, they should share something about their extended selves (for example, family, friends, or associations). For face to face, they should share something about their personal interests or hobbies.

5. Once participants have had time to share information about themselves, repeat the activity so they can begin again with new partners.

People Scavenger Hunt

The People Scavenger Hunt strategy is a quick way to get members of a team talking and interacting as they learn about one another. This simple activity helps establish an environment of discussion and collaboration, which can aid in later activities that require teamwork and team discussion.

Time: 10 minutes

Materials: Topics or characteristics to call during the activity

Description: Use the following steps to implement the People Scavenger Hunt strategy.

1. Put group members in small groups.

2. Call out either a literal item or a characteristic.

3. Each group must send a person with that item or characteristic up to the front of the room as quickly as possible.

4. The first person to tag the designed spot wins the round for the group.

5. Groups can also simply have the person stand and yell something to avoid running around.

6. Items that may be called for include:

   a. Person with the most letters in his or her complete name

   b. Person with the longest shoelaces

   c. When adding up the ages of all siblings, person with the greatest sum

   d. Person who has traveled the farthest

Person or Team Interview

The Person or Team Interview is a common yet useful tool for getting teams who know one other to learn new characteristics.

Time: 10–15 minutes

Materials: List of interview questions on charts or a screen

Description: Use the following steps to implement the Person or Team Interview strategy.

1. Provide some interview questions that either pairs or small teams use to learn about one another. For instance, you might ask questions like:

   a. Where did you graduate from high school?

   b. Where were you born?

   c. What is your least favorite household task?

2. Have teams share one key idea about each person with the larger group.

Variations:

- Have each team member generate an interview question for use with this activity. Once the questions are generated, have the whole group determine which of the questions everyone wants to focus on for the purpose of learning about one another.

- Consider grouping task members according to people's answers (for example, group people who were born in the western United States versus people born in the east).

Pipe Cleaner Metaphors

This creative activity helps establish an environment of discussion and collaboration, which can aid in later activities that require teamwork and team discussion. Participants will use pipe cleaners to create a shape describing themselves or their team.

Time: 10–20 minutes

Materials: Pipe cleaners

Description: Use the following steps to implement the Pipe Cleaner Metaphors strategy.

1. Have participants take a pipe cleaner and form it into something that represents who they are (for example, something they are good at, something they like to do, or something about their family). It can be an actual representation or a symbolic one.

2. When participants are finished, have them pair up with someone and try to guess each other's shape. When a participant's shape is guessed, he or she should explain its connection to his or her identity.

3. Then pull the group together and have people share.

Variations:

- Rather than using a pipe cleaner, participants can do a quick draw or sketch.

- Have teams work together to create pipe cleaner representations of an idea or a response that relates to your presentation. Then, have them present their creation to the group.

Relic Bag

Relic Bag is a wonderful activity to help teammates who work together learn more about one another at deeper levels. This is often best used when you have a group for two or more consecutive days.

Time: 20–45 minutes. Share the activity a day prior to seeing participants, so they have time to collect some relics.

Materials: An example relic (or two) of your own to share

Team Building

Description: Use the following steps to implement the Relic Bag strategy.

1. Participants bring relics from their lives to share.

2. Individual participants get approximately three minutes to share their relics and why they are important to them.

Variations:

- Participants may bring a picture of the relic, rather than the actual item.

- Participants may guess the significance of the relics before the individual describes their importance.

- Challenge participants by allowing them to only obtain a relic from their work bags, phones, or cars.

Say Hello

This efficient greeting activity helps begin conversations within groups through various greetings.

Time: 2–4 minutes

Description: Use the following steps to implement the Say Hello strategy.

1. Group participants.

2. Have each person in the group say hello in a different way.

3. The challenge increases with more people as people search for foreign languages, slang, and gestures to say hi to their fellow group members.

Scavenger Hunt

This well-known teambuilding activity takes on a new twist. Here, participants will work together with their teammates to collect random items requested by the facilitator.

Time: 20 minutes

Materials: Lists of scavenger hunt items (typically including materials most often found on people or in work bags)

Description: Use the following steps to implement the Scavenger Hunt strategy.

1. Present the participants with the following instructions:

   You are about to begin a scavenger hunt with several members of this training group. You may talk with anyone in the group, but you may not leave the room. As you collect items, you must associate each item with the person who gave it to you. You may not get more than two items from any one person.

When your team is finished, your team should loudly announce the phrase "hunt over" to the rest of the group. A prize will be awarded to the team that finishes first.

2. Assign participants to groups (optional), and begin play.

3. Sample scavenger items include:

   a. A driver's license
   b. A family photo
   c. A 1979 or earlier penny
   d. A piece of candy
   e. A planner, personal digital assistant, calendar, or other organizer
   f. A drink
   g. A coffee cup
   h. A marker
   i. A store receipt
   j. A ballpoint pen
   k. A lipstick
   l. A store credit card
   m. A pair of glasses
   n. A magazine or book

Variations:

- Instead of using actual items, list activities and facts as the items to find. For instance, "plays piano." The object of the game is to find someone who plays the piano and associate the person's name with that item.

- Set a timer for a certain number of minutes. The person who has the most items when the timer expires is the "winner." He or she shares the items found and the person with whom they are associated.

Sentence Starters

Sentence Starters is a fun strategy for discovering commonalities—even among teams who know each other quite well.

Time: 5–15 minutes

Materials: Directions for the teams posted on a screen or chart paper

Description:

Use the following steps to implement the Sentence Starters strategy.

1. Team members work to complete a sentence starter that includes everyone on their team. For example: "Our team's favorite food is _____." Everyone on the team must agree.

2. Teams share with the larger group.

Variations:

- Consider a sentence starter that relates to the content for a consensus-building protocol.

- Begin this strategy in pairs, then gradually increase the size of the group to increase the difficulty of the task. Have participants discuss the strategies they used to find an appropriate sentence starter as the groups got larger.

Six Degrees of Separation

Six Degrees of Separation requires small teams to discover commonalities to establish an environment of discussion and collaboration.

Time: 15 minutes

Materials: Prize (optional)

Description:

Use the following steps to implement the Six Degrees of Separation strategy.

1. Have participants find a partner. Have them introduce themselves and make a list of five to ten things that they have in common with each other: where they went to school, year they were born, number of years with the company, food likes, sports likes, and so on.

2. Once they have completed their first list, they must find someone else in the room that also has one of those five to ten things in common with them. When they have found that person, repeat step 1 and develop a new list.

3. Repeat step 2.

4. Continue until participants have met five other people or you call time.

5. Present a prize to the first person able to complete the game.

Tattoo

This strategy allows participants to reveal information about themselves in a creative manner.

Time: 10–20 minutes

Materials: Paper, markers, tape (if you intend to display the pictures)

Description: Use the following steps to implement the Tattoo strategy.

1. Provide participants with the following vignette:

   You have just arrived at Tony's Tattoo Parlor for a tattoo. Tony is competing for "Tattoo King of the Year," a contest sponsored by Needle Knows magazine. Every design is a potential entry, and Tony wants each of his tattoos to say something about the person wearing it. From you, he needs a little inspiration and a design before he can start his work. Tony is excellent at lettering, animals, characters, band logos, maps, and other designs.

   On your piece of paper, you are to design a rough tattoo that reveals something about yourself, your work, your hobbies, or your family, in order to help get Tony's creative juices flowing. You must also make a note about how big the tattoo should be and where you will have it applied.

2. Allow participants time to design their tattoos.

3. Post the papers and share the designs.

Variations:

- Narrow the scope of the tattoo design: for example, what you do at work, an animal most like you, your favorite song, your favorite band, or an adjective that best describes you.

- Divide your group in two. For round one, assign one group the role of Tony and the other group the role of the customer. Each customer must find a Tony and tell him about the design he or she would like and why. Tony is to draw a design, asking questions as he or she goes. After the first set of designs is complete, the groups reverse roles. To encourage additional interaction, ask the customers to "shop around" and find another partner to work with. To debrief, let each Tony describe what he or she drew and for whom.

Theme Song

This collaborative strategy surfaces feeling, tone, and often humor as teams work together to create a theme song. This teamwork and team discussion will aid collegial conversations at later points throughout the training session.

Time: 10 minutes

Description: Use the following steps to implement the Theme Song strategy.

1. Divide participants into smaller groups of three to five.

2. Tell them to share information among themselves until they find a common theme.

3. Once they've got a common theme, have them come up with a song that explains that theme.

4. Have the small groups share their theme song with the larger group. The larger group has to guess the common theme.

Variations:

- Have participants work collaboratively to identify their theme song and write the title of the theme song on a table tent. Then, they share their theme song and its significance with the larger group.

- Have participants or groups of participants select their theme song from a provided list (for example, Disney songs, TV show theme songs, and so on).

Three Numbers

Three Numbers is a quick way to get members of a team talking and interacting about commonalities among the group. This simple activity helps establish an environment of discussion and collaboration.

Time: 5–10 minutes

Materials: Papers, pens or pencils

Description: Use the following steps to implement the Three Numbers strategy.

1. Instruct participants to identify three numbers that have significance to them. Ask them to jot down the three numbers and a few words that explain why they are important numbers.

2. Once adequate time is given, model the share-out.

   "I chose the numbers 3, 6, and 34. I have three grown daughters and six grandchildren, and I have been an educator for thirty-four years."

3. Then ask participants to each share their three numbers and explain their significance.

Two Facts

Two Facts is a quick, fun-filled way to get members of a team discussing unique characteristics about one another. This process can aid in conversations as the teams work together.

Time: 7–15 minutes (depending on group size)

Materials: Pens or pencils, small pieces of paper, a bowl for each team

Description: Use the following steps to implement the Two Facts strategy.

1. This get-to-know-you team builder requires individual teammates to create two facts about themselves.

2. They write them on separate sticky notes or pieces of small paper.

3. They put all the facts in a bowl in the middle.

4. The paper strips are shuffled, and each person collects two pieces of paper from the center.

5. He or she reads one fact and tries to guess whom it represents. Continue until all are completed.

Variations:

- Consider having participants instead write two facts and one lie on their papers. Guess who the participant is and which statement is the lie.

- Consider having participants instead write one fact and one fib on their papers. Guess who the participant is and which statement is the lie.

Who Am I?

Who Am I? is a quick way to get members of a team talking and interacting with one another as they work together to ask questions and then guess a person, place, or thing from the clues provided by their teammates.

Time: 15 minutes

Materials: Premade sticky notes with celebrities, political figures, cartoon characters, and so on written on them

Description: Use the following steps to implement the Who Am I? strategy.

1. For this activity, you will need one sticky note per person.

2. On each note, write the name of a celebrity, political figure, cartoon character, book character, and so on. Each note should have the name of one character.

3. Choose one category or mix it up.

4. Place a sticky note on the back or forehead of each participant.

5. Have participants find a partner and read each other's sticky notes.

6. Tell them they may ask the other person three yes/no questions. Once their questions have been asked and answered, they may make a guess as to their celebrity identity.

7. When participants are correct, have them move the sticky note to their chest. They now become "consultants" who give clues to those still trying to figure out their identities.

8. When they are not correct, have them find a new partner and repeat the process.

   Note: Be sure to choose characters that are appropriate to the age of the participants to avoid "generation gap frustration."

Words in Common

The Words in Common strategy is a process for members of a team to talk about common characteristics. This simple activity helps establish an environment of discussion and collaboration, which can aid in later activities that require teamwork and team discussion.

Time: 5–10 minutes

Materials: Directions posted on the screen or on chart paper, an example to model

Description: Use the following steps to implement the Words in Common strategy.

1. Tell participants that the object of this activity is to generate a list of words or phrases in ninety seconds that represents the group. There are two rules about what is allowed to become part of the list: (1) it must be true about *every* group member; and (2) it must begin with the designated letter.

   Example: The designated letter is D. Group members generated the following list:

   a. Dogs

   b. Denver

   c. Doers

   d. Dynamic

   e. Definitely love kids

2. When the ninety seconds expires, invite a few groups to share the "words in common."

Zip Around

This simple activity helps every team member speak up. This can be especially helpful with some members who are more quiet or reserved, who might be paired with more outgoing and forthcoming participants.

Time: 15–20 minutes

Materials: Premade cards with a question on one side and a response to a different question on the other

Description: Use the following steps to implement the Zip Around strategy.

1. Participants collect one card each.

2. Participant 1 begins by reading the question on his or her card (for example, "Who has _____?") and waits for the participant who has the answer to respond affirmatively. Then, participant 2 says, "Who has _____?" and so on and so forth until all participants have participated.

    Example: One card might say, "Who has the term *reliability*?" The person who has that word on his or her card says, "I have *reliability*." Then he or she reads the question on his or her card: "Who has *assessment fairness*?" The person with that term says, "I have *assessment fairness*. Who has the phrase *common assessment*?"

Chapter 10

Triggering Thinking

In this chapter, you will find nine presentation strategies that focus on *triggering thinking*. You may choose to use strategies to trigger thinking when you want to make connections with your audience to other well-known topics. They are great strategies to stimulate thinking and obtain ideas about a topic already known or vaguely understood before a training. Use these for previewing your content with your audience, uncovering assumptions, and grounding them toward the topic at hand.

Within each strategy, you will find a brief introduction that explains its concept and purpose, a description of the time the activity takes and the materials needed, and a series of steps for implementing the strategy. On occasion, the strategy may also include a couple of variations you may choose to implement, depending on what you wish to achieve with the strategy, the makeup of your group, or the materials available.

Affinity Diagram

An Affinity Diagram is a useful tool for grouping like ideas. This strategy is especially helpful when you are combining needs or questions submitted from a group.

Time: 20–45 minutes

Materials: Notecards or sticky notes, pens or pencils

Description: Use the following steps to implement the Affinity Diagram strategy.

1. Have all members of the group write questions about a topic, or responses to a problem, on notecards or sticky notes.

2. Group the cards or notes by topic.

3. Use the grouped cards or notes to coincide with the direction of the training topics. As you teach a topic, reference the cards or notes that pertain to it.

4. If cards or notes remain, do a question-and-answer session relating to the remaining questions.

    Example: Teams generate one question they want answered about standards-referenced grading. The facilitator collects the sticky notes and groups them according to their topic. Three notes are about conversions to the 100-point scale, five notes are all about modifications for exceptional learners, and so on.

Variations:

* Ask each table to determine one topic or concern that needs to be addressed during the session. This is a great option for obtaining needs from a group. Be mindful that the facilitator or trainer must be very well versed in the topic in order to flexibly address the various needs of the group.

* Seek questions from the group. Group the questions into like categories for referencing throughout the training.

* Solicit summaries from each team. Group the summary statements into an affinity diagram to share out as a culminating activity.

* Consider using these cards or notes to enhance or modify your initial agenda. Please note that trainers and facilitators must be well versed in and experienced with the topic in order to use this strategy to flexibly adjust the initial plan. It is powerful, yet could be concerning, if you lack the experience or knowledge to address what audience teams may seek.

Cooperative Project

Cooperative Project is a process for members of a team to talk about components of the topic. It involves audience members in actively studying or surfacing information about a portion of the training objectives. Using this process will establish an environment of discussion and collaboration, as well as a variation for getting information and ideas into the room.

Time: 15–30 minutes

Materials: Previously prepared topics written on cards or shared via presentation software on the screen, information to provide to participants within a handout or online resources for them to read and discuss

Description: Use the following steps to implement the Cooperative Project strategy.

1. Provide a number of different topic variations to equal the number of groups.

2. Each group draws out a topic, reads and studies the topic, and works as a team to create a mini-presentation to the rest of the group about the topic.

Variations: Cooperative Dialogue

1. Participants number off from 1 to 4.

2. Each participant pairs with another participant from a different group who has the same number to share their respective information. Continue until all group numbers are represented and all groups hear about each delineated section of information.

Fishbowl

Fishbowl is a well-known strategy that allows some audience members to participate directly, while others observe and reflect. It is a great way to instigate thinking about a topic and use a smaller group for the actual conversation.

Time: 15–20 minutes

Materials: Topics for discussion, chairs, paper or small cards for taking notes, pens or pencils

Description: Use the following steps to implement the Fishbowl strategy.

1. Set up a small inner circle of participants to demonstrate an activity for the group. Have all other participants form a larger outer circle around the inner circle of participants.

2. The inner circle (fishbowl) listens carefully to teacher directions and then demonstrates the activity to the rest of the group.

3. As necessary, clarify and correct the activity steps with the fishbowl group.

4. Debrief with the entire group the steps that all groups will follow.

Variations:

- Use the Fishbowl strategy as a type of Socratic seminar, where the inner circle participants participate in a discussion, and the outer circle participants listen and take notes. Later, the outer circle participants can comment on the discussion, using their notes.

- Switch roles so some observers become active within the next discussion of the fishbowl, and those previously active now become observers. Use two or three topics for triggering thinking.

- Conduct mini-fishbowls for large groups within large rooms. Use the same process, yet split the large group into three or four smaller groups with which to conduct a fishbowl experience. If your group is larger than twenty-five, split into two fishbowl groups; if your group is over one hundred, consider four fishbowl groups; and so on.

Four-Symbol Reflection

This strategy allows members of a team to talk about components of the subject that have a metaphorical connection. It involves audience members infusing a feeling with a topic component. Using this strategy will establish an environment of discussion and collaboration, as well as a variation for getting information and ideas into the room that triggered thinking about the focus of the training.

Time: 5–15 minutes

Materials: Prepared reflection template or blank paper, pens or pencils, timer

Description: Use the following steps to implement the Four-Symbol Reflection strategy.

1. Ask participants to divide an 8½" × 11" sheet of paper into quadrants (or provide an already-created template).

2. At the top of each quadrant, participants record one of the following symbols: + Δ ♥ ?

3. Instruct participants to record thoughts and ideas related to each symbol: (1) + = positive thoughts or affirmations; (2) Δ = concerns, challenges, or wonders; (3) ♥ = things you loved about the training; (4) ? = questions still needing to be answered.

4. Using a timer, give participants an opportunity to discuss each quadrant for a few minutes.

5. Ask for reflections for each quadrant from the whole group after discussion time is over.

Graphic Organizers

Using various graphic organizers allows members of a team to talk about components of the subject that have a visual representation in better understanding and discussing them. Using this process will trigger visual organizers with the written ideas and connect your audience at the beginning, middle, and end of training experiences.

Time: Varied

Materials: Precreated graphic organizers that have a direct thinking connection to the topic (for example, Venn diagram for ideas that have unique characteristics as well as some commonalities, or a fishbone organizer for a topic with multiple components that branch out from a single idea)

Description: At the beginning of your presentation, instruct participants to complete a graphic organizer throughout your discussion. Graphic organizers are charts, graphs, or diagrams that participants may complete as they read or view a presentation. There are a variety of ways to use graphic organizers. Some organizers include the following.

- Semantic word map
- Story chart
- Venn diagram
- Spider map
- Network tree
- Word map
- KWL (know, want to know, learn) chart
- Comparison–contrast matrix
- Branching diagrams
- Interval graphs
- Flowcharts
- Matrix diagram
- Fishbone diagram

Variations:

- Hold a group discussion about the graphic organizers.
- Have participants stand up and share their graphic organizers.
- Encourage participants to roam the room and look at each other's graphic organizers.

KTWL Chart

Using KTWL is one specific graphic organizer that connects your audience to trigger existing thinking, questions they need answered, and new learning they obtain throughout a training session. Although a common strategy, it can be especially useful in instigating conversations about what is already perceived and known about a topic. Using this process, as well as the other graphic organizers mentioned previously, connects your audience throughout the training by having them come back to it multiple times.

Time: 5–10 minutes

Materials: Several preprinted pages listing "K-T-W-L" at the top of each of four columns (or paper and pens or pencils, if you wish for the audience to simply draw those columns on a page)

Description: Use the following steps to implement the KTWL strategy.

1. Before reading a selection, hearing a selection, or viewing a video, participants are asked to complete the first three sections of the chart: "What I already know about . . . ," "What I think I know about . . . ," and "What I would like to find out about . . ."

2. After the information has been presented, participants complete the "What I learned about . . ." section.

3. Responses are shared with a partner.

Variations:

- This is also known as a KWL chart.

- Anticipatory guide: Participants are given a series of statements that relate to a reading selection, lecture, or video. Participants indicate *agree* or *disagree*. After the information has been presented, participants check to see if they were correct.

- Extend: Have participants write corrections in their own words.

List-Group-Label

List-Group-Label is a process for members of a team to talk about components of the topic. It involves audience members brainstorming what they already know about a topic. This can also be used later for review and discussion with teams. Using this process will establish an environment of discussion and collaboration, as well as a variation for getting information and ideas into the room.

Time: 10–15 minutes

Materials: Paper, pens or pencils

Description: Use the following steps to implement the List-Group-Label strategy.

1. Have participants individually brainstorm at least six words that have to do with the topic.

2. Instruct participants to pair up, compare lists, and update together to ensure they both have twelve words total.

3. Combine pairs and have them form groups of four, compare words, add to their lists if necessary (up to twenty-four words), then separate their list into four categories (for example, by using a tree map).

4. Invite the teams to develop headings for the categories they create.

Predicting Prose

Predicting Prose is similar to the KTWL Chart activity (page 113), and it connects your audience by triggering ideas already understood as well as the needs of the group. This strategy may serve as a reference to connect your audience throughout the training by having them come back to it for reflection and modifications.

Time: 15–30 minutes

Materials: Pens or pencils, prompts listed on papers or on a screen

Description: Use the following steps to implement the Predicting Prose strategy.

1. Form groups of four.

2. Ensure each group member has a sheet of paper with the team name or number in the corner.

3. Have each person write responses to, "What we want to learn," "What we predict we will do," and "What we hope we walk away with."

4. Give each person one minute to list responses to the prompts.

5. Instruct each person to draw a line after completing his or her ideas.

6. Invite members to share their lists around the team.

7. As each member shares, instruct other members to add new ideas to their lists.

Variations:

- Have small groups take turns standing in a line and reading their possible topics to the whole group. Topics may not be repeated. All participants add new ideas not on their lists.

- Invite groups to pass their papers around and write other ideas onto others' papers.

Word Webs

A Word Web is one specific graphic organizer that connects your audience to trigger existing thinking. Although a relatively common strategy, it can be especially useful in instigating conversations about what is already perceived and known about a topic.

Time: 10–15 minutes

Materials: Chart paper and markers

Description: Use the following steps to implement the Word Webs strategy.

Triggering Thinking

1. Have participants, in a large group, small groups, or individually, begin with a word circled in the center of a large sheet of chart paper.

2. Have them connect the word to related ideas, images, and feelings.

3. Invite groups to share out with other individuals or teams.

Variations: Provide a graphic organizer word web for participants to complete, either as individual participants or as a small group.

Chapter 11

Processing and Practicing

In this chapter, you will find twenty-nine presentation strategies that focus on *processing and practicing*. These activities will help your audience engage in purposeful dialogue, practice the ideas, and consider specific intentions for application and implementation.

Within each strategy, you will find a brief introduction that explains its concept and purpose, a description of the time the activity takes and the materials needed, and a series of steps for implementing the strategy. On occasion, the strategy may also include a couple of variations you may choose to implement, depending on what you wish to achieve with the strategy, the makeup of your group, or the materials available.

Agreement Circles

Agreement Circles are particularly useful when you are seeking levels of agreement. This strategy can be used to develop consensus or simply surface differences in opinion. This strategy also involves a bit of physical movement, which can be useful at times when your audience needs an energy lift.

Time: 5–15 minutes

Materials: Prepared statements relating to the topic

Description: Use the following steps to implement the Agreement Circles strategy.

1. Have participants stand in a circle, facing each other.

2. Make a statement related to the topic.

3. Participants who agree with the statement step into the circle.

4. Then they return to the original circle prior to the facilitator sharing another statement.

5. Repeat for a variety of additional statements.

Variations:

- If there isn't room to form circles, simply have participants raise their hands to agree.

- With a large audience, simply have them tally how many statements with which they agree.

- You could also stand and sit.

Cheers and Fears

Cheers and Fears is a useful protocol for checking about feelings or attitudes related to your topic. It can be used to personalize your training.

Time: 10–15 minutes

Materials: Preconsidered questions you wish to ask the group

Description: Use the following steps to implement the Cheers and Fears strategy.

1. Complete this activity as a big discussion group, or break into two groups.

2. When holding a discussion, ask the group two questions: What are you most excited about with quality assessment ("cheers")? What are you most concerned or apprehensive about ("fears")?

3. Call on volunteers and ask people to explain their responses.

4. Connect the cheers and fears they describe, as well as your own experiences, throughout the training.

Variations:

- Record the cheers and fears on chart paper as they are shared. At the end of the training, ask participants to write a reflection discussing their thoughts and feelings about anything recorded.

- Challenge the group to move a fear into a cheer. Select one to share out.

- Group participants based upon similar cheers or fears for further discussion.

- Group a fear with a cheer about the same question. Allow for dialogue.

Clock Partners

This well-known strategy is most useful with smaller groups (fifty or fewer), and with an audience that will stay throughout the entire time. It doesn't work well if some participants have other obligations that may take them from your training for time periods (such as a meeting obligation or prescheduled phone call). This strategy also involves a bit of physical movement, which can be useful at times when your audience needs an energy lift.

Time: 5–10 minutes

Materials: An analog clock face preprinted or a note-taking page where participants can draw and label an analog clock, pens or pencils

Description: Use the following steps to implement the Clock Partners strategy.

1. Distribute a clock face to each participant with space to write at the 12:00, 3:00, 6:00, and 9:00 spaces.

2. Have the participants walk around and make an appointment with other participants for each of the four time slots. It works best if they begin at 12:00 and work clockwise. Inevitably, there will be a few participants with empty slots.

3. You may have to help ensure everyone's appointments are full by asking whether anyone is missing a clock appointment and facilitating matching participants who need appointments.

4. When it is time for participants to practice with one another, announce, "Find your 12:00 [or 3:00, 6:00, or 9:00] appointment and tell him or her three things: _____."

Variations:

- Record all clock times (1:00–12:00) to use with groups who will reconvene together at later times.

- Allow some groups to consist of groups of three, as different clock times will be left open for different participants. You don't want to spend too long on identifying the partners, as it is more important to keep the participants engaged in discussions with various audience members.

Dramatize Key Concepts

Dramatize Key Concepts is a playful strategy requiring participants to collaborate to create a dramatic inference from the ideas learned. This strategy also involves a bit of physical movement, which can be useful at times when your audience needs an energy lift.

Time: 10–20 minutes

Materials: Preconsidered components shared on a screen for teams to select from or to be assigned to act out

Description: Have a randomly organized group of participants or small teams nonverbally act out concepts to improve their comprehension. For instance, a group may elect to nonverbally act out norms in a professional learning community or key terms discussed, or they may want to demonstrate a dramatic way to depict informal assessment.

Variations:

- Model mathematical or scientific concepts that teachers may teach (for instance, photosynthesis, the earth's rotation and revolution around the sun, covalent or ionic bonds in chemistry, improper fractions, and the like).

- Randomly call out teams to demonstrate their dramatization and allow the rest to guess the topic.

- Have one team act out their concept for another team nearby.

Elbow or Shoulder Partners

Most are familiar with *turning to a person near you* to discuss content. This is a simple tool for providing voice and obtaining feedback that can be used in your trainings.

Time: 2–7 minutes

Description: Use the following steps to implement the Elbow or Shoulder Partners strategy.

1. After practicing the discussion process, ask participants to turn to an elbow partner to discuss feedback they would offer to an anonymous sample of participant work.

2. Once participants have brainstormed their feedback suggestions with a partner, have them verbalize in front of the whole group in order to build confidence and deepen understanding.

3. Engaging participant voices in group discussions around quality feedback deepens content knowledge and helps participants learn from one another.

Variations:

- Turn to a new partner.

- Take one idea shared.

- Set a timer to equalize the amount of time each person gets to talk.

Fan and Pick

In this strategy, teams use cards to discuss various focused topics or questions. There is an element of surprise that is engaging and fun, and it stimulates discussion about objectives from your training.

Time: 15–20 minutes

Materials: Premade question cards

Description: Use the following steps to implement the Fan and Pick strategy.

1. Divide participants into teams, and give each team a set of premade question cards.

2. Have participant 1 "fan" the cards. Participant 2 picks a card and reads the question. Participant 3 answers the question. Participant 4 paraphrases and praises the answer or offers help. Then a new person takes the cards and becomes the "fanner."

Gallery Walk

In this cooperative learning strategy, the instructor devises several questions or problems and posts each question or problem at a different table or at a different place on the walls (hence the name "gallery"). Teams move to different tables or places around the room to read, discuss, pose questions, and add information for the important pieces of the training.

Time: 15–25 minutes

Materials: Preconsidered topics or questions for reaction and reflection, chart paper, markers

Description: Use the following steps to implement the Gallery Walk strategy.

1. Divide participants into as many groups as there are questions or topics.

2. Invite each group to move from question/topic to question/topic.

3. At each point, have groups read, react, and write their response(s) on the chart.

4. After writing the group's response to the first question or topic, the group rotates to the next position, adding to what is already there.

5. At the last question, it is the group's responsibility to summarize and report to the group.

Variations:

- In order to vary the writing, have groups switch markers as they rotate. This way, a different person writes on each chart.

- You may elect to repeat critical questions, thus having four chart focus areas which are then repeated. This way, you can abbreviate the time frame by not having nine to ten different discussion points. You will also have some teams who share the same discussion topic. They can meet up to share both charted ideas and then combine the thinking prior to sharing with the larger group.

Give and Get

In this whole-group activity, participants have a task—to give and to get information. They walk around the room and randomly select partners with whom to share information and get new information about an assigned topic. This is a great strategy for helping participants learn from one another as well as from you.

Time: 7–10 minutes

Materials: Paper or an organizer with "Give" listed in one area and "Get" listed in another, pens or pencils

Description: Use the following steps to implement the Give and Get strategy.

1. Before beginning, give participants quiet time to consider what they know about a particular topic, and to record a number of possible responses (sketches, words, phrases, or sentences) on a sheet designed for that purpose.

2. Pose a question that is open-ended enough to generate a range of responses, or provide a worksheet with multiple questions to discuss and about which to respond.

3. Point out the resources (charts, articles, books, and so on) available to help participants generate ideas or find responses.

4. Then allow a couple of minutes for participants to record their ideas.

5. Provide a set amount of time (about six to eight minutes) to get up and find a groupmate with whom to share ideas.

6. Partners ask for clarification about any detail not understood, comment on anything of interest, then select one idea from the other's list and add it to their own, with their partner's name next to it.

7. When one exchange is completed, participants move on to a new partner.

8. At the end of the exchange period, the teacher facilitates a group debriefing of ideas.

Variations:

- A volunteer is asked to share one new idea from a conversation partner, utilizing the language structure of reporting, such as:

  - I learned from _____ that _____.

  - I found out from _____ that _____.

  - _____ said (mentioned) that _____.

  - My partner, _____, told me (said that) _____.

- The participant whose idea has just been reported shares the next idea gleaned from another conversation partner, and the process continues.

In-Text Questions

This strategy is useful for quiet reflection. You will provide written information with imbedded questions for reflection. Participants reflect and then can discuss with others.

Time: 10–20 minutes

Materials: Reading excerpts, precreated in-text questions related to your topic (for instance, if you were having them read about various knowledge application processes, you might have a question that reads, "How might you summarize this process?" Later throughout the reading, you may ask, "What is a topic you teach where this strategy would be useful?" Even later, you might ask, "Think of how you might vary this idea for the grade level or content area you teach.")

Description: Use the following steps to implement the In-Text Questions strategy.

1. Create questions designed to guide participants through the reading and provide a purpose for reading.

2. Participants preview these in-text questions, then answer them as they read the article.

3. Participants review their answers with their small group, and then share them with the whole group.

Lines of Communication

This strategy infuses repeated practice in a low-stress situation to give shy or reluctant participants more confidence to share and take risks. It also imbeds physical movement to adding energy back into the room.

Time: 10–20 minutes

Materials: Predrafted prompts; bell, musical cue, chime, or other signal

Description: Use the following steps to implement the Lines of Communication strategy.

1. Give a prompt or ask a question.

2. Have participants stand in two rows facing each other.

3. Invite participants to take turns responding to the prompt with the person standing across from them, and then discuss together for thirty seconds to one minute.

4. When time is up, give a signal (using a bell, a musical cue, chimes, or another signal). Have participants wrap up their comments or discussion and move one position to the left. The participant at the end of one of the lines who is left without a partner moves down the center aisle to the far position of the opposite line to find a new partner.

5. Find a new prompt and repeat the procedure until everyone has had a chance to share with every other member of the group, or as long as interest and focus remain.

Mentimeter

This technological tool is an easy way to include the use of phones, tablets, or computers in a productive manner. After creating questions or prompts, the facilitator shares the link and then asks audience members to respond in real time.

Time: 10–12 minutes

Materials: Internet access to www.menti.com; prepared questions to which participants will respond

Description: Use the following steps to implement the Mentimeter strategy.

1. Pose a question and decide on the format for the group responses (word cloud, multiple-choice responses, speech bubbles).

2. Have participants log on to www.menti.com. They will access the response format via a code.

3. Have participants then share their responses.

4. Visualize the responses on the screen.

Variations:

- Use this process in a pre–post manner. Ask participants to respond to a question or prompt at the beginning of a learning opportunity. After the learning occurs, have participants respond to the same survey to see if change has occurred among group members.

- Divide participants into groups, and compare the responses between groups.

Numbered Heads Together

This routine is effective when participants are solving problems or responding to questions that have a specific right answer. It is also useful in rotating the person who speaks to the larger group.

Time: 10–15 minutes

Materials: Predetermined questions or prompts about your topic posted on a screen or chart paper

Description: Use the following steps to implement the Numbered Heads Together strategy.

1. Group participants in teams of four, and have each participant number off from 1 to 4.

2. Ask the participants to complete a task, engage in an activity, or answer questions.

3. Participants put their heads together to discuss the answer for a set amount of time. They must make sure everyone on the team knows the answer.

4. Randomly call a number from 1 to 4 (use a spinner, draw a number card, or roll a die).

5. On each team, the participant whose number was called writes down the answer.

6. When all teams are ready, have the designated participant stand and share his or her team's response.

7. Check each team's answer for accuracy.

Pantomime

This strategy is similar to Dramatize Key Concepts (page 119), and is most useful with groups that are a bit more playful in nature, as it requires them to collaborate to create a pantomime from the ideas learned. This strategy also involves a bit of physical movement, which can be useful at times when your audience needs an energy lift.

Time: 10–15 minutes

Materials: Predetermined key concepts or ideas ahead of time that are relatively easy to act out

Description: Use the following steps to implement the Pantomime strategy.

1. Assign each group a key concept or idea about which to pantomime.

2. Have groups prepare their assigned topic (three minutes).

3. Be certain all group members are involved.

4. Invite other teams to guess which key concept or idea is being depicted.

Reader Response Chart

This is an independent activity that encourages participants to consider what they have learned and reactions or connections of their own. Because this is a solo strategy, it can balance self-study and reflection with the myriad of team discussions that may have occurred.

Time: 10–12 minutes

Materials: Paper, pens or pencils

Description: Use the following steps to implement the Reader Response Chart strategy.

1. Have participants draw a T-chart on their paper.

2. On the left side, they write three interesting, informational learnings.

3. On the right side, participants respond to the information with their own reactions, memories, questions, something to learn more about, or comparing and contrasting something else they know that is related or a variation of the idea. For instance, a teacher may think that two-column note taking is similar to Cornell notes, yet requires a summary statement that he or she had not considered with Cornell notes.

4. Have participants come back to their initial thinking later in the learning for additional review or revisions.

Variations:

- Have participants complete the left side of the T-chart, then exchange their paper with another person, who is given the opportunity to respond to the information recorded. Once another person records his or her responses, instruct the two people to converse about the information.

- Participants may use the Reader Response Chart in combination with Clock Partners (page 119). After locating their 3:00 partner, they share one idea from each side of the Reader Response Chart.

Review Meal

This can be an independent activity or a team activity. Review Meal encourages participants to consider what they have learned throughout the training and categorize them into smaller ideas to more substantial learnings obtained.

Time: 10–15 minutes

Materials: Paper plates, pens or pencils

Description: Use the following steps to implement the Review Meal strategy.

1. Pass out the paper plates.

2. Each person or team creates a metaphoric meal pertaining to the content. The appetizer is one small thing used to fine-tune a practice. The entrée includes three key ideas important to remember. The dessert is an ending idea or process to replicate.

Role-Play

This strategy is useful when participants need to practice applying a process like a coaching conversation. Here, small teams practice an interaction or conversation with one another, reflect, and consider areas warranting increased practice.

Time: 15–30 minutes

Materials: Topics and process steps listed on a screen

Description: Use the following steps to implement the Role-Play strategy.

1. Invite pairs of learners to sit facing one another.

2. Have participant 1 conduct the practice process or strategy.

3. Have participant 2 listen and participate.

4. Repeat the process by interchanging roles.

Variations:

- Form small groups and give each group member a piece of paper and a pencil. Each paper has a different but related question or topic on it (for example, social reasons to immigrate, economic reasons to immigrate, and political reasons to immigrate). Have participants write a short answer about their question or topic and pass the paper to the next participant. Continue until all participants have written on all papers in their group. Ensure all participants stay simultaneously engaged.

- Rotate role-play partners for increasing practice with the process and skills two or three times.

Round Table

This cooperative strategy is a great one to have participants review ideas or notes from others within their group. It is especially useful in reviewing important concepts as it exemplifies reviewing and processing learning for various team members.

Time: 10–12 minutes

Materials: Paper, pens or pencils

Description: Use the following steps to implement the Round Table strategy.

1. Ask a question that has many possible answers.
2. In groups, have the participants make a list of possible answers by one at a time saying an answer out loud and writing it down on a piece of paper.
3. The paper is then passed to the next participant to record another answer.
4. The process continues until the facilitator or trainer tells the participants to stop.

Roving Reporter

This interactive process involves teams obtaining fresh ideas from other teams about the same topic. It is useful for processing information deeply and considering various perspectives.

Time: 10–15 minutes

Materials: Predetermined problems or action plans created by teams

Description: Use the following steps to implement the Roving Reporter strategy.

1. Have participants work as teams to solve problems or create implementation action plans.
2. Instruct one participant from each group to move around gathering discoveries, ideas, angles, approaches, pathways, and so forth from other groups.
3. That participant shares any new ideas with his or her original team to augment the original plan.

Spaces

This practicing strategy asks participants to group with others beyond their own tables.

Time: 15–20 minutes

Materials: Predetermined questions for groups to consider, questions for discussion at each breakout space

Description: Use the following steps to implement the Spaces strategy.

1. Pose a question or share a reaction to a topic. For example, educators may determine a grade level or class with which to try a new idea (K–2, 3–5, 6–8, or 9–12).

2. Have participants write their choice and rationale.

3. Invite participants to go to the space of the room representing their choice. For example, if participants intend to use this idea with primary students, have them go to the K–2 group.

4. In their space, participants pair up and share their reasons for selecting that space.

5. Small groups break apart within the space and discuss the idea and how they might use it with their selected age group.

Variations:

- To facilitate brainstorming, post different concepts around the room and have participants travel to add information or list everything they know about it.

- To facilitate a content review, label the four corners of the room with *Disagree*, *Strongly Disagree*, *Agree*, and *Strongly Agree*. Read a controversial statement and have participants go to the corner representing their point of view. All participants sharing a point of view work together to collect evidence and present an argument supporting their beliefs.

Stir the Group

This processing and practicing strategy is a great way to mix up existing groups and to obtain new ideas. Only specific people will leave an existing group to move into another for a brief conversation. Ultimately, the person who moved returns with new ideas.

Time: 15–20 minutes

Description: Use the following steps to implement the Stir the Group strategy.

1. Number off within teams (1–4).

Processing and Practicing

2. Pose a question. Discuss responses with the original team.

3. Ask a number to move one team clockwise. Discuss ideas.

4. Ask a number to move one team counterclockwise. Discuss a new question.

5. Repeat as you like.

Table Family

This is a simple tool for providing voice and obtaining feedback that can be used in your trainings. Use this idea for brainstorming the participants' feedback or suggestions with their team prior to verbalizing in front of the whole group in order to build confidence and deepen understanding.

Time: 4–15 minutes

Materials: Specifications of roles and the responsibilities for each displayed on a screen

Description: Use the following steps to implement the Table Family strategy.

1. Provide teams time to select roles (for example, facilitator, speaker, and writer).

2. Periodically use those roles to engage in group conversations.

Variations:

• Take one idea shared to the large group.

• Set a timer to equalize the amount of time each person gets to talk.

• Assign roles to each table family member (speaker, facilitator, timer, norms monitor, and so on).

Taboo Review

This interactive practicing activity is an engaging way for participants to more deeply describe components learned from the training.

Time: 10–15 minutes

Materials: A set of "taboo" cards. Each card should list a term or concept as well as three or four "forbidden" words that participants are not allowed to utter. The forbidden words should be words related to the topic. For example, if you were trying to describe the term "reliability," you can't use words or phrases like "consistent" or "same." This encourages participants to think deeply about their understanding of a topic.

Description: Use the following steps to implement the Taboo Review strategy.

1. Divide participants into teams, and select one person in the team to go first.

2. This person must try to get his or her team to guess the term or concept in less than thirty seconds (you may want to increase or decrease the time limit, depending on how long it actually takes the group—the point is to get the participants to succeed, but add an incentive of bearing the clock).

3. To do so, they must stand in front of the team and say as many clues as possible. However, the taboo words cannot be used in any of the clues, or the team's turn will be over automatically.

4. Alternate turns until all of the words have been defined.

Take a Stand

Take a Stand is similar to Agreement Circles (page 117), but involves less movement. Here, participants respond to yes-or-no or agree-or-disagree statements. It is useful when determining the level of controversy or variations in feelings about specific ideas.

Time: 5–10 minutes

Materials: Preplanned questions to ask

Description: Use the following steps to implement the Take a Stand strategy.

1. Teacher poses a yes-or-no or agree-or-disagree question.

2. Participants stand up for *yes* if they agree, and sit down for *no* if they disagree.

Variations:

- Participants practice pronouncing words or phrases by using a combination of clapping their hands, hitting the table, and snapping their fingers. In round-table style, each member uses a word from the list, in the order given, in a sentence to create a collaborative story.

- Participants might be allowed to crouch to indicate some agreement and some disagreement. For those in the crouched position, the facilitator asks one person standing (agreement) and one person sitting (disagreement) to spend one minute to try to persuade the crouched participants to take a different stand. Revote on the topic to see if agreement or disagreement increased.

Talking Stick

This strategy gets participants processing a topic by rotating a *talking stick* to signify when one turn is over and the other begins.

Time: 5–10 minutes

Materials: Several rain sticks or other objects

Description: Use the following steps to implement the Talking Stick strategy.

1. Designate an object as the *talking stick* and have participants pass it around the group—first clockwise and then at random.

2. Give a prompt and ask members to number or letter off among their tables (1–4, A–C). Then, indicate the number or letter of the group member to begin.

3. The first participant with the talking stick speaks while everyone listens.

4. The participant then passes the object to the left. The process continues until everyone in the group has had a chance to speak or until the teacher gives a signal to stop.

5. Participants can pass (decline to respond) only once. This allows reluctant speakers to hear others in their small group before contributing.

Variations:

- To extend the activity, once everyone in the group has had a turn speaking, anyone in the group may ask for another turn by saying something like "I'd like to add another thought. Please hand me the talking stick."

- The trainer or facilitator may randomly select a letter and a group to "have the stick" and share with the larger group.

Talking Turns

This is a simple tool for providing more equalized voice within table groups during processing discussions, and to prevent one person monopolizing the conversation time.

Time: 5–15 minutes

Materials: Objects you will use to represent the turn for talking (pennies, paper clips, or sticky notes work well)

Description: Use the following steps to implement the Talking Turns strategy.

1. Ensure each teammate has one or two talking turns.

2. Divide objects (slips of paper, sticky notes, or paper clips) to represent a talking turn among members of the team.

3. Each time a person in the team speaks, he or she must put one of the talking objects into the center.

4. When all of one's objects are gone, that person is exempt from contributing until all others have had a chance.

Variations:

- Use coins to "spend" when speaking. When you have spent the total amount each person gets (4 cents, in pennies; 20 cents, in dimes; and so on), you must wait until all have spent their amounts before divvying the coins up to spend again in another discussion (Kagan, 1994).

- Use the objects throughout the day to extend the period of time more voices must be present during discussions. In other words, discussion begins with those who still have a penny, sticky note, or paper clip.

- Divide the objects after one processing activity to allow a fresh use of the talking objects prior to the next reflecting protocol.

Think Aloud

During Think Aloud, participants say out loud what they are thinking about when reading, solving problems, or simply responding to questions. It allows individual processing first prior to doing so with the larger team. This is especially useful when modeling a skill or procedure that has multiple steps.

Time: 5–10 minutes

Materials: Model a problem-solving example (for example, draft an action-planning item through the template you might be using)

Description: Use the following steps to implement the Think Aloud strategy.

1. Model a think-aloud (when the facilitator is speaking aloud as he or she models the steps in the process learned) to demonstrate practical ways of approaching difficult problems while bringing to the surface the complex thinking processes that underlie the process. It might sound like, "As I am completing the first portion of the action-planning template, I want to consider the strategy I am going to use. Next, I consider an approximate time frame, so I will say 'fall of 2019.' Then, I consider what training might be needed, and I fill that in here."

2. Participants team up and practice using a similar strategy on a new question or problem.

Think-Write-Pair-Share

This popular discussion activity ensures that participants are practicing key concepts in partners and small groups, and can be done multiple times during a training. It is a great way to process an idea thoroughly.

Time: 15–20 minutes

Materials: Paper, pens or pencils, predetermined discussion prompts shared on a screen or chart paper

Description: Use the following steps to implement the Think-Write-Pair-Share strategy.

1. Letter off the participants (A, B, C, and D) within groups of four (all groups should have A, B, C, and D).

2. Pose a discussion prompt and model a response using the content.

3. Think–Write: Give participants silent think time to jot down their response.

4. Pair–Share: At the signal, partners A/B and C/D read their responses to each other and discuss.

5. To further structure this time, you may wish to signal when it is time for each partner to share. This prevents one partner from dominating or using all of the discussion time, and ensures that both partners have the opportunity to discuss their responses.

6. Add additional practice by having A share with C, and B with D. Or, have the two pairs share with each other after they have discussed their ideas individually.

7. An additional variation is to have participants record their partner's response.

8. Keep the pace brisk enough to prevent dead time. It's better for partners to have a little less time than they need, rather than too much.

9. Signal for the group to reconvene and invite volunteers to share their responses with the larger group.

Variations: It may be helpful to include additional parameters in the directions, such as the following.

- Identify similarities and differences between your responses.

  - My idea is similar to (elaborates on, is like, complements) _____'s idea.

  - We both think that _____. However, I also think _____.

- Combine your responses to generate a more complete (compelling, accurate) response, such as the following.

  - Between the two of us, we came up with _____.

◆ After some discussion, we decided (agree, have come to the conclusion) that _____.

• Generate a list of remaining questions.

• Use these clarifying statements in your discussion by asking questions like the following.

◆ How did you decide that _____?

◆ In other words, you think that _____. Is that right?

◆ I'm not sure what you mean by _____. Can you please explain?

Word or Concept Sorts

Sorting concepts and key words is a wonderful practicing activity. It can be an active way to have participants use the information you provide and process the intricacies.

Time: 10–15 minutes

Materials: Words, phrases, or concepts written out on small cards

Description: Use the following steps to implement the Word or Concept Sorts strategy.

1. Prepare words or phrases on strips of paper.

2. Have the participants organize the strips according to meaning, similarities in structure, derivations, sounds, words, and phrases related to a content concept or other criteria determined.

3. Share out ideas.

Variations:

• Ask participants to write a short paragraph using as many of the words or phrases as they can.

• Combine paragraphs from one team with those of another to create a longer and more inclusive summary.

Zip Line

Zip Line is a new twist on the familiar Nonverbal and Verbal Lineup strategy (page 139). During this version, participants will process and practice key terms or topics with others in the group. It also involves physical movement, so it can increase the energy of the group.

Time: 10–15 minutes

Materials: One set of cards with terms or topics, and another set of cards with definitions or descriptions

Description: Use the following steps to implement the Zip Line strategy.

Processing and Practicing

1. Provide each participant with one card.

2. Instruct participants to find and stand next to the person who has the matching topic or definition.

Variations:

*   Once participants find their word-definition partner, they work together to write a sentence that appropriately uses the word.

*   Ask multiple groups to combine to create a paragraph depicting key ideas and concepts.

*   Ask participants to create the topics on blank cards (one card has the topic, another a key definition or related idea) and distribute them prior to the connecting portion of the activity.

Chapter 12

Consensus Building

In this chapter, you will find four facilitation strategies that focus on *consensus building*. You may choose to use consensus-building strategies when you need a group to converge thinking about an idea or when you want to create a common vision or set of beliefs about a topic. These activities will help your audience coalesce independent ideas into collective group actions.

Within each strategy, you will find a brief introduction that explains its concept and purpose, a description of the time the activity takes and the materials needed, and a series of steps for implementing the strategy. On occasion, the strategy may also include a couple of variations you may choose to implement, depending on what you wish to achieve with the strategy, the makeup of your group, or the materials available.

Dot Voting

This idea, also known as Spend-a-Buck (Kagan, 1994), is an effective tool to ensure all participants have equal opportunity to listen and learn ideas. You can also use it to increase prioritization preferences regarding an activity list or project for the group.

Time: 30–45 minutes

Materials: Colored sticky dots (enough for four per person), chart paper, markers, predetermined options or options that emerge from the group to be written onto the charts

Description: Use the following steps to implement the Dot Voting strategy.

1. Prior to voting, brainstorm (or have the participants brainstorm) a list in regard to a question prompt (such as "What are the best ways to give one another feedback?").

2. Notate all possible solutions to the question on one large poster paper.

3. Give each participant three sticky dots, and have them place their dots beside the solutions they feel should be prioritized. Any combination of dots is allowed—in other words, one participant might elect to put all of her dots on one option, whereas another participant may divvy up his dots among three different options.

4. Total the points for each option, and identify those with the highest point values as the priority actions for the group. When participants see that their vote counts, they are more engaged in their learning.

Variations:

- Use small sticky notes or even written check marks or stars if you do not have dots. The key is for participants to have something to place onto a chart in order to signify prioritization.

- This tool can also be used electronically.

GOILS: Groups of Increasingly Large Size

This protocol allows facilitators to methodically obtain questions, concerns, or ideas from a large group and distill them down to a manageable number for consideration (ideally, three). Facilitators can then respond to those questions, concerns, or ideas for pondering. This process ensures all participants have a chance to develop their understanding of a topic and to see what happens when that understanding is synthesized with the thinking of others.

Time: 20–30 minutes, depending upon the size of the group

Materials: Notecards or sticky notes for the topics or questions, pens or pencils

Description:

1. Identify a topic for discussion.

2. Have participants find a partner. Instruct the partners to take turns discussing the relevance of the topic for two minutes.

3. Invite partnerships to then spend one minute identifying three points to share.

4. Have each pair find another pair to group with. The partnerships both share their three sharing points, so that groups then have a total of six points. Through discussion, groups should condense those six points into three main points.

5. Instruct each foursome to find another foursome to group with. Invite the groups to repeat this process, ending again with three main points.

6. Have groups repeat this process until the whole large group has decided on three main points.

7. Document these three points to use or review later.

Idea Survivor

Idea Survivor is an effective tool to provide participants with opportunities to share ideas and ultimately decide upon those from a team that are "best" to move actions forward. Teams prioritize their preferences and move limited amounts forward to the larger group. Ultimately, those ideas that survive are those that originated within groups and seemed worthy for the larger group's consideration.

Time: 20–30 minutes

Materials: Predetermined questions for teams to consider, charts or note-taking paper, pens or pencils

Description: Use the following steps to implement the Idea Survivor strategy.

1. Share important ideas or questions with the participants. Collect a list of their ideas.

2. Have participants rank order the ideas (either individually or in a small group).

3. Ask participants to identify the top ten ideas within the team. Then, have them identify the top five ideas within the team. Finally, ask them to select the top three ideas within the team.

4. Invite all teams to bring their top three ideas to the larger group.

Nonverbal and Verbal Lineup

Nonverbal and Verbal Lineups are processes for sharing differing perspectives and building collective thinking or consensus among the group.

Time: 10–20 minutes

Materials: Paper, pens or pencils, chart paper, markers

Description: Use the following steps to implement the Nonverbal and Verbal Lineup strategy.

1. Instruct the entire group to line up according to a specific criterion (for example, age, birthday, first letter of name, or distance traveled to school).

2. Have the participant at the end of the line lead the line until he or she is standing opposite the head of the line. Have participants pair up until each person has a partner.

3. Invite small teams to discuss opposing ideas and hear differing perspectives.

4. After completion of the partner discussions, combine pairs into quads or sextets.

5. Ask these newly formed groups to draft statements of agreement among this new group.

6. Merge these agreements onto chart paper or electronically, and offer suggestions to the larger group that encompass the agreed-on statements. This might sound like, "What each group mentioned in their statements was 'Children need guidance,' and 'We have to be willing to modify our thinking.' Let's combine these two ideas into, 'We need to modify our thinking to provide students with the guidance they need.' Can we all agree upon that collective statement?"

Variations:

• This is called "folding the line" or "split the line." Teams of four members can then be formed from this lineup.

• You may also elect to use a model group to simply demonstrate the structure.

Ranking

The Ranking strategy is a process for prioritizing key concepts or ideas independently first and then within larger groups.

Time: 15–20 minutes

Materials: List of items, paper, pens or pencils

Description: Use the following steps to implement the Ranking strategy.

1. Ask participants to individually rank items in a list from least important to most important.

2. Place individuals in small groups or pairs. Have each group or pair discuss the list and reorder once both are in agreement.

3. Continually increase the group sizes as needed to come to either small team or larger group consensus.

4. Allow the top rankings to provide options within the consensus building of the large group. For instance, you might recognize that all groups had three particular ideas in their top five. Ask the group if they can all agree that those are most important to all groups. Then, discuss the common statements each group had in the top eight. Continue until the group establishes some areas of agreement.

Chapter 13

Summarizing

In this chapter, you will find twenty-two presentation strategies that focus on *summarizing*. You may choose to use summarizing strategies when you want to reinforce the infusion of ideas, information, strategies, and processes you have taught in your presentation. These processes and protocols help your groups determine the key ideas from the less important details and synthesize the learning as application into their practices.

Within each strategy, you will find a brief introduction that explains its concept and purpose, a description of the time the activity takes and the materials needed, and a series of steps for implementing the strategy. On occasion, the strategy may also include a couple of variations you may choose to implement, depending on what you wish to achieve with the strategy, the makeup of your group, or the materials available.

3 As

The 3 As strategy helps your audience direct their summarization into something that affirmed their thinking, another idea they acquired, and a question they may still need to ask. It frames it so all are appropriate and even expected.

Time: 15 minutes

Materials: List of the 3 As displayed on a screen

Description: Use the following steps to implement the 3 As strategy.

1. Mix the group. Standing partners works well.

2. Play music while participants move.

3. Stop the music as participants group into teams of two or three.

4. Respond to the 3 *A* questions:

    a. Affirm

    b. Acquire

    c. Ask

3-2-1

The 3-2-1 strategy helps participants summarize their understanding, surface a question or concern that still exists, and transfer learning to new situations.

Time: 10–20 minutes

Materials: Paper, pens or pencils

Description: Use the following steps to implement the 3-2-1 strategy.

1. Participants jot down three ideas, concepts, or issues presented.

2. Participants jot down two examples or uses of the idea or concept.

3. Participants write down one unresolved question or a possible confusion.

Variations:

-   2-2-2
-   1-1-1

A-B-C Summarize

The A-B-C Summarize strategy is an engaging way for participants to use the letters of the alphabet to begin a summary of a key concept.

Time: 10–15 minutes

Materials: Paper, pens and pencils

Description: Use the following steps to implement the A-B-C Summarize strategy.

1. Assign each participant in a group a different letter of the alphabet, and have him or her select a word or short phrase, or draw a picture starting with that letter, that is related to the topic being studied.

2. Repeat as needed.

Variations:

-   Conduct as a *whip-around* where subsequent participants have to share out their thinking.

- Say a key idea that starts with the next letter of the alphabet (for example, participant 1 states an idea starting with *A*, participant 2 states an idea starting with *B*, and so forth).

Across-the-Room Allies

This is a simple tool for summarizing information, sharing a connection for use, and providing voice and obtaining feedback that can be used in your trainings.

Time: 5–10 minutes

Materials: None

Description: Use the following steps to implement the Across-the-Room Allies strategy.

1. Have participants mingle and then connect with one to two others who aren't at their tables.

2. Invite participants, in their new groups, to process ideas, share new ideas, and gain feedback.

Variations:

- Add music while participants move across the room. When the music stops, they group and discuss.

- Create teams of four to six people, and have each share an idea in a round-robin fashion.

Folder Categorizing

This strategy is great for solidifying understanding around key vocabulary or key phrases, or for categorizing topics. Here, each small team is provided a folder with permanently labeled topics on one side and descriptions or applications on the other. Small teams categorize them to summarize their understanding. The folders can be used multiple times with different groups.

Time: 10–15 minutes

Materials: File folders, sticky notes, sticky labels

Description: Use the following steps to implement the Folder Categorizing strategy.

1. Create folders that include categories about a topic on the left side. Those categories are permanently affixed with sticky labels. Provide the topics, words, or ideas to be categorized on the right side, one per sticky note, in no particular order.

2. Have participants categorize the sticky notes from the right side underneath the appropriate category label on the left side. For instance, the left side may have affixed categories of informal and

formal assessments. The various example topics on the right side might include examples like probing conversations, written quiz, common assessment, use of Plickers or whiteboard responses, and so on.

Variations:

- Have participants categorize vocabulary, community workers, modes of transportation, physical attributes (shape), and so on. Provide every three to four participants a set of about thirty-five to forty cards (vocabulary, pictures, and so on). Have groups lay the cards face up on the table. As participants pick up a card, have them name it and then place it in a category. Once the participants have placed all the cards into a category, they should be able to state the name of the category in a complete sentence.

- For advanced groups, ask them to also state the category and provide a rationale.

  ◆ These are _____.

  ◆ These are _____ because _____.

Getting the Gist

This strategy is great for solidifying understanding around key vocabulary or key phrases, or for determining importance from print materials.

Time: 15–20 minutes

Materials: Chart paper, markers, printed text, prize (optional)

Description: Use the following steps to implement the Getting the Gist strategy.

1. Participants read a section of printed text.

2. After reading, ask participants to underline ten or more words or concepts that are deemed "most important."

3. List the words on the chart paper or using presentation software.

4. Teams write a summary statement or two, using as many of the listed words as possible.

Variations:

- Write a topic sentence to precede summary sentences.

- Have participants work to use as many words or concepts as they can throughout the training. Keep track if you like for the most used in response to questions or during discussion. Award a prize if preferred.

Information Puzzle

This strategy is great for solidifying understanding around key vocabulary, key phrases, or important topics. Participants work with limited information, and combine efforts with others in order to summarize all the pieces of the puzzle. This is an interactive strategy that also involves team building and physical movement.

Time: 20–30 minutes

Materials: Informational text parceled onto puzzle pieces

Description: Use the following steps to implement the Information Puzzle strategy.

1. Each participant (in a group) has one or two pieces of information needed to solve the puzzle, but not all the necessary information.

2. Participants must work together to share information in order to complete the puzzle.

In the Bag

In the Bag is great for summarizing understanding around key vocabulary, key phrases, or important topics. Participants randomly obtain a topic and must share their thinking about the topic. This is an interactive strategy that also involves team building.

Time: 10–15 minutes

Materials: Bags with premade questions, or topics to be placed inside one or more bags

Description: Use the following steps to implement the In the Bag strategy.

1. Provide each team with a bag, or use one bag for the entire group.

2. Participants take turns pulling out a topic and sharing their learning or ideas about it.

3. You can also sprinkle in some fun topics.

Examples:

- Why (your topic) is important to learn
- A key takeaway
- An idea you will share with others
- My idea of a perfect day
- A fun way to travel
- The best job in the world

- The greatest book ever written
- My favorite Olympic sport
- How to clean a bedroom in ten minutes
- The best place in the world to live
- A great gift
- The most important invention

Mystery Words

Mystery Words is similar to In the Bag (page 145), as it is great for summarizing understanding around key vocabulary or key phrases. One partner provides clues about a key word or phrase in order for his or her partner to guess it. The team works through a small list of words provided on the screen. This is an interactive strategy that is quite engaging.

Time: 10 minutes

Materials: Two to four lists of words related to the training shared on a screen

Description: Use the following steps to implement the Mystery Words strategy.

1. Ask for a volunteer to sit in a chair facing his or her small group, but with his or her back to the word listed so the target vocabulary cannot be seen.

2. Have the small group describe the listed word, and allow the volunteer to guess the word or phrase.

Variations:

- Group participants into dyads or triads for increased involvement.

- Provide the teams with a cue for celebrating when they successfully complete the list.

One-Minute Paper

This independent strategy is great for providing quiet time for participants to summarize key information.

Time: 5–10 minutes

Materials: Blank piece of paper or a note-taking page from a handout, pens or pencils

Description: Use the following steps to implement the One-Minute Paper strategy.

1. Decide on a focus or topic for the paper. You may choose to ask participants, "What was the most important thing you learned?"

2. Provide one minute for participants to write.

3. Discuss the results with teams or as a large group.

Variations:

- This could also be used to answer questions. Use this prompt: What important question remains unanswered?

- Consider a roundtable format. After participants write for a few minutes, ask them to stop writing and rotate their papers clockwise around the group. Instruct each participant to read what was written, then add to that person's thinking. On completion, the originator gets back his or her paper with additional ideas generated from teammates.

Picture This

This independent strategy is similar to One-Minute Paper. It is great for providing quiet reflective time for participants to summarize key information through pictures.

Time: 15–20 minutes

Materials: Blank sheet of paper or chart paper

Description: Use the following steps to implement the Picture This strategy.

1. Have participants fold or draw lines on their paper or chart paper to divide it into eight sections.

2. Have participants draw pictures or symbols to represent words or major concepts. Participants are not to label the drawings.

3. Invite participants to exchange papers or posters with other teams.

4. Ask the new team to try to correctly label the other's drawings.

Posters

Posters is an interactive protocol for helping groups summarize major topics presented. The facilitator selects the type of drawing requested, shares it with the team, and seeks informative, picture-like products that demonstrate understanding of presented material.

Time: 20 minutes

Materials: Poster paper, markers

Description: Use the following steps to implement the Posters strategy.

1. Have participants work in teams to create posters to depict the topic. These may include:

   a. *Illustrated Timeline*—Tell the plot or sequence on a timeline, with pictures that depict the events.

   b. *Movie Poster*—Advertise the content from a training by creating a movie poster complete with ratings, pictures, actors, descriptions, and comments by a critic.

   c. *Comic Strip*—Create a six-panel comic strip of the content.

     d. *Image and Quote*—Choose an image and a quote from the lesson content that are *representative or important*. The poster should include a title.

     e. *Advertisement*—Choose an item from the lesson content and make a newspaper or magazine ad for it.

2. Invite participants to share out their posters with at least one other group.

Variations:

- Have groups travel gallery-walk style, with sticky notes in hand, and discuss both the highlights of each poster (the *wow*) and a lingering question they have (the *wonder*).

- Each group posts one wow and one wonder.

- Once rotations are complete, each group is to write a summary of the wows and wonders on their poster and choose at least one question to address orally.

Quick Draw

This independent strategy is similar to One-Minute Paper (page 146). It is great for providing quiet reflective time for participants to summarize key information through a picture.

Time: 5 minutes

Materials: Blank sheet of paper or sticky note, pens or pencils

Description: Use the following steps to implement the Quick Draw strategy.

1. Provide a prompt. This might be "What is a key takeaway for you?" or "What will be an important idea or concept for you to implement?"

2. Have participants complete a quick draw on a sheet of paper.

3. Ask for volunteers to share with others. Note: Some adults are apprehensive about sharing their drawings, so see variations for options.

Variations:

- Quick write—prereading or prewriting focus activity. Ask participants to respond to a question or prompt in writing for five minutes. The emphasis should be on getting thoughts and ideas on paper.

- If participants get stuck, instruct them to repeat phrases over and over until a new idea comes to mind.

- Assessment strategy—have participants write for two to three minutes about what they learned. This could be an open-ended question from the facilitator.

Reciprocal Teaching

This interactive, multistep process gets participants discussing information from printed text.

Time: 15–20 minutes

Materials: Passages to be prepared and shared

Description: Use the following steps to implement the Reciprocal Teaching strategy.

1. Ask two participants to work together to read a passage.

2. Each may have a text, or they may share a text.

3. Ask participant 1 to read one paragraph aloud.

4. Ask participant 2 to summarize the paragraph in his or her own words.

5. Have the participants repeat the process in reverse.

Roundabout

This summarizing protocol helps participants review key content or pose questions using anonymity when answering to create a nonthreatening atmosphere in which all participants have an equal chance to share their ideas. It encourages all participants to interact through reading and writing.

Time: 10–15 minutes

Materials: Chart paper, markers, sticky notes

Description: Use the following steps to implement the Roundabout strategy.

1. Have participants write different but related questions or prompts on chart paper posted around the room.

2. Invite participants to move around the room either freely or in small groups and write ideas or construct answers on each paper. Alternately, have them record the ideas on sticky notes ahead of time and then post the notes on the appropriate papers.

3. Share and process the ideas with the whole group with a gallery review (participants silently move from poster to poster, reading and noting important ideas), small-group to whole-group presentations, or some other technique.

Summarizing

Variations:

- Roundabout brainstorming—give each small group a poster with a title related to the topic. Instruct each group to use a different-colored marker to list four or five strategies or activities that relate to their topic. Have participants rotate to all the other posters, reading them and adding two or three more strategies. Then, have them discuss the results. Switch writers as the team revolves from poster to poster.

- Have teams create a prompt for the next team to summarize. Pass that topic to a new team, and have the new team formulate summarizing statements about it.

Six- or Twelve-Word Summary

This efficient protocol helps individuals coalesce their summaries into limited numbers of words. Each group creates a different summary, and sharing is optional.

Time: 5–15 minutes

Materials: Paper, pens or pencils

Description: Use the following steps to implement the Six- or Twelve-Word Summary strategy.

1. Have participants work individually or as teams to create six or twelve words that summarize important aspects of a particular chunk of instruction or reading.

2. Share out as time allows.

Variations:

- If the group size allows, it works well to hear every summary. Ask representatives from each group to come up front and form a line facing the audience. Beginning with the person on the far left, have all groups share their summary. If a microphone is used, it is passed to the right to ensure each summary is heard easily. Following all of the shares, invite applause.

- Consider limiting the words even more (maybe three to five words only).

Teams Check

Teams Check helps participants review key content and pose relevant questions to others.

Time: 15–20 minutes

Materials: Notecards or strips of paper, pens or pencils

Description: Use the following steps to implement the Teams Check strategy.

1. Group participants, and give each group a different question about the training topic about which to respond.

2. Have participants individually complete a response to the proposed question.

3. Next, instruct the participants to pass their question and response clockwise around their team table.

4. Invite the others in the group to add to the responses.

5. Keep rotating and responding until all group members contribute to each other's responses.

Three-Step Interview

This routine is effective when participants are responding to questions that do not have a specific right answer. It is a useful process for obtaining summarized comments and perspectives from the group.

Time: 20–30 minutes

Materials: List of issues to discuss

Description: Use the following steps to implement the Three-Step Interview strategy.

1. Present an issue about which varying opinions exist and pose several questions for the group to consider.

2. Have participants work in pairs. One is the interviewer; the other is the interviewee. Each interview should last two to three minutes.

3. At the signal, have partners switch roles.

4. After individual sets of partners have interviewed each other, have them pair with another set of partners.

5. Each partner shares his or her partner's idea with the others.

Variations: Depending on your goals for the work, you may—

- Have the groups of four synthesize their ideas and list commonalities and differences on a chart to be posted and shared orally, or as a gallery walk, so participants can read each other's ideas.

- Invite several participants to share their own or their partner's ideas as you chart them. As you go, have participants indicate agreement with a thumbs-up. Once you have collected a few distinct ideas, ask whether there are any other ideas not yet reflected.

Summarizing

- Use these charts as a basis for asking participants to write a summary of the interview results.

- Have group participants letter off (A, B, C, and D). Invite them to use the following interview steps in order to share what they have written in a quick write until they all have been read.

  Step 1: A interviews B; C interviews D.

  Step 2: B interviews A; D interviews C.

  Step 3: A interviews C and D about B; B interviews C and D about A; C interviews A and B about D; D interviews A and B about C.

- Assign an interview topic that relates to the unit theme ("What is your favorite character in _____, and why?") and have participants select partners. First, one partner interviews the other. Second, they reverse roles. As a next step, several pairs (depending on group size, the number or pairs can range from three to six) form a group and do a round-robin to share their opinions.

Two Cents

Two Cents is a process to provide closure for a group or team through sharing summarized comments.

Time: 15–20 minutes

Materials: Pennies (enough for two per participant)

Description: Use the following steps to implement the Two Cents strategy.

1. Introduce the activity by talking about how everyone has contributed his or her two cents throughout the training.

2. Give every participant two cents, and share that each is to give away the two cents to other individuals in the group.

3. To give away a penny, participants must say a positive quality that they have admired about the individual to whom they are giving it.

4. The activity works well as a round-robin activity so everyone can hear who each other recognizes, or as a free-for-all format where individuals get up at once and share individually with people.

5. The goal is for participants to try to give away all their pennies, even the ones they receive.

Whip Around

This strategy is a common protocol to summarize learning and allow everyone's voice to be heard.

Time: 10 minutes

Materials: Predetermined questions for reflection and summary of key content, paper, pens or pencils

Description: Use the following steps to implement the Whip Around strategy.

1. Pose a question that encourages participants to reflect on a response.

2. Have them jot down two or three possible responses utilizing frames that you have provided.

3. Whip around the room, having each participant share one of his or her responses.

Variations:

1. To prepare, generate thirty questions (or enough so that there is one per participant). Write two questions on a card (questions 1 and 2 on one card, questions 2 and 3 on the next card, questions 3 and 4 on the next card, and so on).

2. Distribute one card to each participant, and permit time for everyone to jot a response to the first question on his or her card. Participants may work in partners to help each other generate a response.

3. Begin with a volunteer who reads the question and response. Then have this person ask, "Who has the question . . . ?"

4. The person with that question states the response and asks, "Who has the question . . . ?" Continue until everyone has contributed.

Work Sample Review

This strategy allows participants to summarize the results of a longitudinal sample of work.

Time: Varies

Materials: Preprepared guiding questions

Description: Use the following steps to implement the Work Sample Review strategy.

1. Come up with a guiding question, such as, What does the work reveal about the following?

   ◆ The purpose of the task

- How critical thinking skills are developing through experiences

- The writing process

- Responsibility, choice, and citizenship

- Connections being made between others' lives and their learning

- Opportunities for creativity and self-expression

- Experiences in applying what they learn to new situations

2. Decide on a sampling strategy. For example, collect all work for one day, or collect the work of four to six participants for two to five days. (Select participants who are representative of different ability levels, cultures, genders, and races.)

3. Identify the methods for the collection of work. For example, what kinds of work will be collected: written papers, artwork, audiotapes, participant journals, homework, work in context or divorced from the assignment or discussion, or another type.

4. Decide on the duration of the slice—for example, one day, a day and a half, or one week.

5. Obtain envelopes or boxes for each participant's work. Have participants place only their first names on their work.

6. Decide if you want to share your insights from the slice with anyone and how this will take place.

Variations:

- Use participant work and the corresponding reflective questions.

- Trainers or facilitators may use this idea for self- or team reflection.

Writing Tweets

Tweets are a 21st century practice that can function as a wonderful summarizing tool. Pairs work to summarize the meeting or learning experiences in less than 280 characters.

Time: 10–15 minutes

Materials: Paper and pens or pencils, computer with internet access

Description: Use the following steps to implement the Writing Tweets strategy.

1. Provide models of tweets used to summarize.

2. Have participants work in pairs to write a tweet.

3. Invite pairs to share out their tweets. Ask the group to vote on the most effective one.

Chapter 14

Checking for Understanding

In this chapter, you will find seven presentation strategies that focus on *checking for understanding*. You may choose to use strategies to check for understanding when you want to ensure your audience members clearly understand the information you share. These activities will help elicit questions, concerns, or needed clarifications from the audience in order to gain the most from your session.

Within each strategy, you will find a brief introduction that explains its concept and purpose, a description of the time the activity takes and the materials needed, and a series of steps for implementing the strategy. On occasion, the strategy may also include a couple of variations you may choose to implement, depending on what you wish to achieve with the strategy, the makeup of your group, or the materials available.

Confidence Hand Responses

The process of Confidence Hand Responses is a quick and easy way to check the assurance of your participants about information you have presented. Here, audience members simply use hand signals to share a rating of confidence.

Time: 5–10 minutes

Materials: None

Description: Use the following steps to implement the Confidence Hand Responses strategy.

1. Make a statement or ask for confidence in understanding by asking for verbal and nonverbal comprehension checks ("hand

pointing up for very confident," "hand flat [parallel to the ground] for so-so," and "hand pointing down" for no confidence in understanding).

2. Use throughout discussions as needed.

Variations:

- Thumbs up, thumbs middle, thumbs down
- Green cards, yellow cards, red cards

Muddiest Point

The protocol of Muddiest Point encourages participants to share something about which they are not certain (in other words, a bit muddy). Collect muddy points from teams in order to efficiently yet thoughtfully address areas for clarification.

Time: 2–5 minutes

Materials: Paper, pens or pencils

Description: Use the following steps to implement the Muddiest Point strategy.

1. Ask participants to write down the muddiest points in the training (up to that point, what was unclear) and share with other team members.

2. Teams bring forth the one or two muddiest points for clarity.

Parking Lot Tool

This commonly known protocol allows you to check understanding by asking participants to voice opinions; comment, ask questions, or request information without interrupting what is going on at the time. This feedback tool allows participants to provide feedback, and allows the trainer or facilitator to monitor learning, respond to needs in the group, and celebrate learning successes.

Time: Not specified

Materials: Chart paper, marker, sticky notes

Description: Use the following steps to implement the Parking Lot Tool strategy.

1. Hang a large sheet of paper divided into four quadrants: Plus, Delta, Questions, and Ideas.

2. Encourage participants to write their questions and comments in the corresponding quadrants of the chart (or on sticky notes, which they then place on the chart) at break times or as needed.

3. During work sessions or breaks, check the chart and answer or comment on each point.

4. Relay the information to the group as a whole, or allow for ano-nymity as it suits the needs of the group.

Send-a-Question

The Send-a-Question process allows teams to work together to answer questions or solve problems posed by other teams. It is a great way to elicit more ideas than your own for clarifying information solicited from you or checking for understanding with the group.

Time: 15–30 minutes

Materials: 3 x 5 notecards, pens or pencils

Description: Use the following steps to implement the Send-a-Question strategy.

1. Invite each participant on a team to make up a review question or potential problem and write it on a 3" × 5" card.

2. Have the writer ask the question of the other members of the team. When everyone agrees on an answer, the writer should record it on the back of the card.

3. The teams then send their card to another team. Teams respond by having one participant read the first question.

4. Each team member writes down an answer. Team members then compare and discuss their answers. If they agree, they turn the card over to see if they concur with the sending team. If not, they write their answer on the back of the card as an alternative answer.

5. Have a second participant read the next question, and so on.

6. Send the stacks of cards to a third, then a fourth, group until all teams have had a chance to answer all questions.

7. When the cards return to the senders, provide an opportunity to discuss and clarify.

Signal Cards

Signal Cards is a variation on Confidence Hand Responses (page 155). This is a rela-tively quick and easy way to check the assurance of your participants about information you have presented. Here, audience members simply use colored cards to correspond to a level of confidence in their understanding of material presented.

Time: 1–5 minutes

Materials: Colored cards or index cards (green, yellow, pink)

Description: Use the following steps to implement the Signal Cards strategy.

1. Create cards to check for understanding. Green means "I've got it," yellow means "I'm not sure, maybe," and pink means "I'm lost. I have questions."

2. Monitor the audience and pause to clarify or respond to questions as they raise them in the air as asked, or at any point when something isn't understood.

Snowball

This engaging strategy helps you check for the understanding of individual participants. During this process, participants rate their understanding, put that rating onto a small piece of paper, and throw that paper (a snowball) toward an area of the room. Participants find someone else's snowball, collect it, read it, and share out. The facilitator clarifies any concern noted.

Time: 10–15 minutes

Materials: Small pieces of white paper, pens or pencils

Description: Use the following steps to implement the Snowball strategy.

1. Have each participant write a question on a small sheet of paper, then crumple it into a ball shape.

2. Ask participants to number off by 1 and 2.

3. Call for all 1s to stand in one line and all 2s to stand across from them.

4. The 1s are to throw their "snowball" across to the 2s.

5. The 2s are to pick up one snowball, read the question, then try to respond to the question their partner posed.

6. Then, repeat the process where the 2s throw and the 1s catch, read, elaborate, and seek clarification.

Tickets to Enter or Exit

Check for understanding using this classroom strategy of entry and exit tickets. Here, the leader poses a question or prompt to seek understanding of the topic from the group. Participants respond and share their enter or exit tickets after break, before lunch, or whenever needed to provide evidence of understanding.

Time: 5–10 minutes

Materials: Index cards

Description: Use the following steps to implement the Tickets to Enter or Exit strategy.

1. Ask participants a specific question about the lesson.

2. Have participants respond on the index cards (their tickets). Collect these tickets either on their way out or on their way in the next day.

3. Evaluate the need to reteach or revisit questions that need to be answered.

Variations:

- Participants list what they have learned and how they might apply it to their situations.

- Participants list interesting ideas, strategies, or concepts learned throughout the training.

- Participants could also list a question that they have or need answered the following day (in multiday trainings).

Conclusion

Success is no accident. It is hard work, perseverance,
learning, studying, sacrifice and most of all, love
of what you are doing or learning to do.

—Pelé

You have acquired a public speaking opportunity. It might have been for new teachers, parents, certain groups of teachers, or seasoned administrators. Now what?! This resource is intended to help take the mystery out of planning, delivering, and troubleshooting a presentation, and engaging your participants. My belief is that there is both an art and a science to presenting ideas well. The science is infused through the practical tools provided for preparing your message, from questions you ask yourself, to a quadrant that helps guide you through the needs of audience members. The science continued through over one hundred suggested processes and protocols, not only detailing their use but also providing a match between strategies presenters may use and the goal for the group. Do you need to check for understanding, or have your participants summarize their thinking? Regardless of your need, there are protocols to assist you in taking that group where they might need to go.

The art of presenting is really in the delivery, tips, tricks, and troubleshooting ideas. Here, I peeled back the onion to surface very specific approaches for dynamically delivering your message. I presented ideas that fluctuated from how to arrange a room for effective interaction, to introductions of yourself and your topic, to centering yourself for optimal performance. Additionally, I offered various tactics for setting up parameters for successful group interactions through dealing with inappropriate behaviors. All in all, if you needed one book for helping you more effectively work with adult audiences, this is it! My hope is that this resource will assist you from your planning and preparation, to delivery, professionalism, and reflection. Go, be better tomorrow than you were today!

Appendix

The following is a listing of tech supports to assist you with imbedding more gizmos into your presentations. Included is a plethora of tools for group processing, obtaining feedback, photo editing, seeking images, designing charts, and so forth.

- **Google Docs (www.google.com/docs/about) and Microsoft Office Track Changes:** Allow trainers or facilitators to provide electronic comments in real time, keeping the feedback both specific and timely

- **Clicker or Plickers technology (www.plickers.com):** Allow users to provide immediate feedback to learners

- **Padlet (https://padlet.com):** Allows facilitators to create an electronic bulletin board filled with additional resources obtained by using a unique Padlet link

- **iPiccy (http://ipiccy.com):** Contains many powerful and easy-to-use photo editing tools within an internet browser. Users can auto-adjust photos in one click, or crop, rotate, and resize images in no time. iPiccy contains over one hundred photo effects and pro-level photo enhancements, facial retouching, and frames

- **ThingLink (www.thinglink.com):** Tags images, videos, and 360° media with instant access to additional information, audio, video, embeds, and web links

- **Easelly (www.easel.ly):** Acts as a simple infographic maker that lets users visualize any kind of information

- **The Noun Project (https://thenounproject.com):** Includes two million icons for reference
- **Infogram (https://infogram.com):** Helps users create beautiful charts, maps, graphics, and dashboards
- **Poll Everywhere (www.polleverywhere.com):** Uses multiple-choice questions to identify gaps in understanding or kick off group discussions with a colorful word cloud. Users can invite participants to respond simultaneously by visiting a website or texting a number on their phones. Responses appear in an animated graph or chart embedded in your presentation. Results update live for all to see
- **BigHugeLabs (https://bighugelabs.com):** Helps users do innovative things with digital photos, like posters, pop art, and magazine covers
- **Delivr (delivr.com):** Helps users easily design and use QR codes
- **WeVideo (www.wevideo.com):** An online video editor that makes it easy to capture, create, view, and share movies at up to 4K resolution for playback anywhere

See www.howspace.com/resources/digital-facilitation-tools for more information and details about some of these tech resources, in addition to others.

References and Resources

Access Center: Improving Outcomes for All Students K–8. (2007). *Professional development modules*. Washington, DC: U.S. Department of Education, Office of Special Education Programs. Accessed at www.air.org/project/access-center-improving-outcomes-all-students-k-8 on August 6, 2019.

Adamo, J. (2014). *Full spectrum success: Living and leading in true color*. Scotts Valley, CA: CreateSpace.

Allen, R. (2008). *TrainSmart: Effective trainings every time* (2nd ed.). Thousand Oaks, CA: Corwin Press.

Bangert-Drowns, R. L., Kulik, C. C., Kulik, J. A., & Morgan, M. (1991). The instructional effect of feedback in test-like events. *Review of Educational Research, 61*(2), 213–238.

Blair, H. (2018, November). *ARTiculate Real&Clear*. Presented at the National Speakers Association Colorado Conference, Denver, CO.

Blanton, B. (2009). *How to deliver the talk of your life*. Accessed at http://sixminutes.dlugan.com/how-to-deliver-talk-life/ on April 19, 2019.

Boulet, M.-M., Simard, G., & de Melo, D. (1990). Formative evaluation effects on learning music. *Journal of Educational Research, 84*(2), 119–125.

Bowman, S. L. (2009). *Training from the back of the room! 65 ways to step aside and let them learn*. San Francisco: Pfeiffer.

BrainyQuote. (n.d.a). *A place for everything quotes*. Accessed at www.brainyquote.com/quotes/benjamin_franklin_109062 on July 23, 2019.

BrainyQuote. (n.d.b). *First impressions quotes*. Accessed at www.brainyquote.com/quotes/malcolm_gladwell_395749?src=t_first_impressions on April 17, 2019.

BrainyQuote. (n.d.c). *George Jessel quotes*. Accessed at www.brainyquote.com/quotes /george_jessel_392909 on April 18, 2019.

BrainyQuote. (n.d.d). *Pele quotes*. Accessed at www.brainyquote.com/quotes/pele_737774 on April 19, 2019.

BrainyQuote. (n.d.e). *Visual quotes*. Accessed at www.brainyquote.com/topics/visual on July 23, 2019.

Brookfield, S. (1995). Adult learning: An overview. In A. Tuinjman (Ed.), *International encyclopedia of education*. Oxford: Pergamon Press. Accessed at https://pdfs .semanticscholar.org/2a84/6b46cebfebbfe7873702562993be2109251b.pdf on July 23, 2019.

Brookfield, S. (1996). *Understanding and facilitating adult learning: A comprehensive analysis of principles and effective practices*. San Francisco: Jossey-Bass.

Brookhart, S. M. (2008). *How to give effective feedback to your students*. Alexandria, VA: Association for Supervision and Curriculum Development.

Brookhart, S. M. (2017). *How to give effective feedback to your students* (2nd ed.). Alexandria, VA: Association for Supervision and Curriculum Development.

Browning, G. (2006). *Emergenetics: Tap into the new science of success*. New York: HarperCollins.

Burton, V. (2016). *Successful women speak differently*. Eugene, OR: Harvest House.

Butler, R., & Nisan, M. (1986). Effects of no feedback, task-related comments, and grades on intrinsic motivation and performance. *Journal of Educational Psychology, 78*(3), 210–216.

Butler, D. L., & Winne, P. H. (1995). Feedback and self-regulated learning: A theoretical synthesis. *Review of Educational Research, 65*(3), 245–281.

Carless, D. (2006). Differing perceptions in the feedback process. *Studies in Higher Education, 31*(2), 219–233.

Comana, F. (2015, February 20). *Strengthening your communication skills with clients* [Blog post]. Accessed at https://blog.nasm.org/newletter/strengthening-communication -skills-clients/ on April 19, 2019.

Continenza, D. (n.d.). *This is the cheapest time of day to book a flight*. Accessed at www .southernliving.com/travel/cheapest-time-of-day-to-book-a-flight on July 23, 2019.

Csikszentmilhalyi, M., Rathunde, K., & Whalen, S. (1993). *Talented teenagers: The roots of success and failure*. New York: Cambridge University Press.

DiResta, D. (2018, April 7). *Public speaking success secret: Stay in your lane* [Blog post]. Accessed at www.diresta.com/knockoutpresentationsblog/public-speaking-success -secret-stay-in-your-lane on April 17, 2019.

DiResta, D. (2019). *Knockout presentations: How to deliver your message with power, punch, and pizzazz*. New York: Morgan James.

Duarte, N. (2012). *HBR guide to persuasive presentations.* Boston: Harvard Business School.

Dunst, C. J., & Trivette, C. M. (2009). Let's be PALS: An evidence-based approach to professional development. *Infants and Young Children, 22*(3), 164–176.

Dunst, C. J., & Trivette, C. M. (2012). Moderators of the effectiveness of adult learning method practices. *Journal of Social Sciences, 8*(2), 143–148.

Dutro, S. (2009). *Systematic English language development: A handbook for secondary teachers.* Vista, CA: E.L. Achieve.

Dweck, C. S. (2007). The perils and promises of praise. *Educational Leadership, 65*(2), 34039.

Eggert, M. A. (2010). *Brilliant body language: Impress, persuade and succeed with the power of body language.* Upper Saddle River, NJ: Pearson.

Ericsson, K. A., Krampe, R. T., & Tesch-Römer, C. (1993). The role of deliberate practice in the acquisition of expert performance. *Psychological Review, 100*(3), 363–406.

Feinstein, S. (Ed.). (2006). *The Praeger handbook of learning and the brain* (Vol. 2). Westport, CT: Praeger.

Feltovich, P. J., Prietula, M. J., & Ericsson, K. A. (2006). Studies of expertise from psychological perspectives. In K. A. Ericsson, N. Charness, R. R. Hoffman, & P. J. Feltovich (Eds.), *The Cambridge handbook of expertise and expert performance* (pp. 41–67). New York: Cambridge University Press.

Fisher, D., & Frey, N. (2007). Implementing a schoolwide literacy framework: Improving achievement in an urban elementary school. *The Reading Teacher, 61*(1), 32–45.

Fisher, D., & Frey, N. (2012). Making time for feedback. *Educational Leadership, 70*(1), 42–47.

Garmston, R. J., & Wellman, B. M. (2009). *The adaptive school: A sourcebook for developing collaborative groups* (2nd ed.). Norwood, MA: Christopher-Gordon.

Hattie, J. (2009). *Visible learning.* New York: Routledge.

Hattie, J., & Timperley, H. (2007). The power of feedback. *Review of Educational Research, 77*(1), 81–112.

Heflebower, T. (2005). *An educator's perception of STARS from selected Nebraska Education Service Unit staff developers.* Unpublished doctoral dissertation, University of Nebraska–Lincoln. Accessed at http://digitalcommons.unl.edu/dissertations /AAI3194116/ on December 27, 2008.

Heflebower, T. (2018a). *Presenting perfected: Dynamic delivery.* San Bernardino, CA: Amazon.

Heflebower, T. (2018b). *Presenting perfected: Planning and preparing your message.* San Bernardino, CA: Amazon.

Heritage, M. (2008). *Learning progressions: Supporting instruction and formative assessment.* Washington, DC: Council of Chief State School Officers.

Herrmann, N., & Herrmann-Nehdi, A. (1996, 2015). *The whole brain business book: Unlocking the power of whole brain thinking in organizations, teams, and individuals* (2nd ed.). New York: McGraw-Hill.

Hunter, D. (2007). *The art of facilitation* (2nd ed.). San Francisco: Jossey-Bass.

Hunter, D., Bailey, A., & Taylor, B. (1995). *The art of facilitation: How to create group synergy* (North American ed.). Tucson, AZ: Fisher.

Jensen, E. (1998). *Trainer's bonanza: Over 1000 fabulous tips and tools.* San Diego, CA: The Brain Store.

Kagan, S. (1994). *Cooperative learning.* San Clemente, CA: Kagan.

Kagan, S., & Kagan, M. (2004). The structural approach: Six keys to cooperative learning. In S. Sharan (Ed.), *Handbook of cooperative learning methods* (pp. 115–133). Westport, CT: Greenwood Press.

Karia, A. (2012). *How to deliver a great TED Talk: Presentation secrets of the world's best speakers.* Scotts Valley, CA: CreateSpace.

Karia, A. (2015). *How to design TED-worthy presentation slides.* Scotts Valley, CA: CreateSpace.

Karia, A. (2017). *100 keys for powerfully persuasive presentations.* Accessed at www .slideshare.net/CommunicationSkillsTips/100-keys-for-powerfully-persuasive -presentations on September 19, 2019.

Kluger, A. N., & DeNisi, A. (1996). The effects of feedback interventions on performance: A historical review, a meta-analysis, and a preliminary feedback intervention theory. *Psychological Bulletin, 119*(2), 254–284.

Knowles, M. S., Holton, E. F., & Swanson, R. A. (Eds.). (2012). *The adult learner: The definitive classic in adult education and human resource development* (7th ed.). New York: Routledge.

Kolb, D. A. (1984). *Experiential learning: Experience as the source of learning and development.* Englewood Cliffs: Prentice Hall.

Kolb, D. A. (2015). *Experiential learning: Experience as the source of learning and development* (2nd ed.). Upper Saddle River, NJ: Pearson Education.

Liimatainen, H. (2018). *25 best digital facilitation tools for consultants.* Accessed at www .howspace.com/resources/digital-facilitation-tools on July 29, 2019.

Likert, R. (1932). A technique for the measurement of attitudes. *Archives of Psychology, 22*(140), 5–55.

Lipton, L., & Wellman, B. (2016). *Groups at work: Strategies and structures for professional learning.* Melbourne, Victoria, Australia: Hawker Brownlow Education.

Martin, S. (2007). *Born standing up: A comic's life.* New York: Scribner.

Marzano, R. J. (2006). *Classroom assessment and grading that work*. Alexandria, VA: Association for Supervision and Curriculum Development.

Marzano, R. J. (2012). *Becoming a reflective teacher*. Bloomington, IN: Marzano Resources.

Marzano, R. J., & Haystead, M. (2008). *Making standards useful in the classroom*. Alexandria, VA: Association for Supervision and Curriculum Development.

Nuthall, G. A. (2005). The cultural myths and realities of classroom teaching and learning: A personal journey. *Teachers College Record, 107*(5), 895–934.

Obama, M. (2018). *Becoming*. New York: Crown.

Pappas, C. (2013). *The adult learning theory—andragogy—of Malcolm Knowles*. Accessed at https://elearningindustry.com/the-adult-learning-theory-andragogy-of-malcolm -knowles on April 19, 2019.

PBS. (2007). *Mirror neurons*. Accessed at www.pbs.org/wgbh/nova/education/body/mirror -neurons.html on April 19, 2019.

Peterson, D. (2018). *5 principles for the teacher of adults*. Accessed at www.thoughtco .com/principles-for-the-trainer or facilitator-of-adults-31638?print on April 19, 2019.

Pike, R. W. (1994). *Creative training techniques handbook: Tips, tactics, and how-tos for delivering effective training* (2nd ed.). Minneapolis, MN: Lakewood Books.

Pike, R. W. (2003). *Creative training techniques handbook: Tips, tactics, and how-tos for delivering effective training* (3rd ed.). Amherst, MA: HRD Press.

Rall, J. (2017, November 8). *Active learning in the adult classroom, part 1*. [Video file]. Accessed at www.floridaipdae.org/index.cfm?fuseaction=resources.ABE&cagiid =1A38432D290E67EF5344020E15DAB9AB15D8D8EFC9B52A2772A87DA2 BBE07267 on September 19, 2019.

Rath, T. (2007). *StrengthsFinder 2.0: Discover your CliftonStrengths*. New York: Gallup Press.

Reynolds, G. (2010). *Presentation Zen design: Simple design principles and techniques to enhance your presentations*. Berkeley, CA: New Riders.

Saphier, J. (2005). Masters of motivation. In R. DuFour, R. Eaker, & R. DuFour (Eds.), *On common ground: The power of professional learning communities* (pp. 85–113). Bloomington, IN: Solution Tree Press.

Schön, D. A. (1983). *The reflective practitioner: How professionals think in action*. New York: Basic Books.

Schön, D. A. (1987). *Educating the reflective practitioner: Toward a new design for teaching and learning in the professions*. San Francisco: Jossey-Bass.

School Reform Initiative. (n.d.a). *Compass points: North, south, east, and west—An exercise in understanding preferences in group work*. Accessed at https://schoolreforminitiative .org/doc/compass_points.pdf on April 18, 2019.

School Reform Initiative. (n.d.b). *Protocols*. Accessed at www.schoolreforminitiative.org /protocols/ on April 19, 2019.

Solem, L., & Pike, B. (1997). *50 creative training closers*. San Francisco: Jossey-Bass.

Solomon, M. R., Hughes, A., Chitty, B., Marshall, G., & Stuart, E. (2005). *Marketing: Real people, real choices* (4th ed.). Upper Saddle River, NJ: Prentice Hall.

Stronge, J. (2007). *Qualities of effective teachers*. Alexandria, VA: Association for Supervision and Curriculum Development.

Thorndike, E. L. (1913). *Educational psychology, Volume I: The original nature of man*. New York: Columbia University, Teachers College.

Tough, A. (1999). *The adult's learning projects: A fresh approach to theory and practice in adult learning*. Toronto, Ontario, Canada: Ontario Institute for Studies in Education.

Tuijnman, A. C. (Ed.). (1996). *International encyclopedia of adult education and training*. Oxford, England: Pergamon Press.

University of Pennsylvania. (2009). *Visual learners convert words to pictures in the brain and vice versa, says psychology study*. Accessed at www.sciencedaily.com/releases /2009/03/090325091834.htm on July 23, 2019.

Vogt, M., & Echevarría, J. (2008). *99 ideas and activities for teaching English learners with the SIOP model*. Boston: Pearson.

Waehner, P. (2019). *Maximum heart rate formula for women*. Accessed at www.verywellfit .com/womens-heart-rate-response-exercise-3976885 on July 23, 2019.

Weller, S., & Herrmann, N. (1996). *Quadrant*. Accessed at http://thepeakperformancecenter .com/educational-learning/learning/preferences/the-brain/hbdi/ on April 19, 2019.

Wikipedia. (n.d.). *Margaret Wolfe Hungerford*. Accessed at https://en.wikipedia.org/w /index.php?title=Margaret_Wolfe_Hungerford&oldid=850406224 on July 23, 2019.

Wild, J. L. (1999, January). *Thread #3: Teambuilding and communication—Facilitation, coaching, mentoring, and training—Understanding the differences*. Paper presented at the 99th conference of the International Association of Facilitators, Williamsburg, VA.

Wilkinson, M. (2004). *The secrets of facilitation: The S.M.A.R.T. guide to getting results with groups*. San Francisco: Jossey-Bass.

Zakhareuski, A. (n.d.). *15 secrets to teaching adults*. Accessed at https://busyteacher .org/7273-teach-adults-15-secrets.html on April 19, 2019.

Zoller, K., & Landry, C. (2010). *The choreography of presenting: The 7 essential abilities of effective presenters*. Thousand Oaks, CA: Corwin Press.

Index

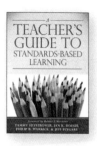

A Teacher's Guide to Standards-Based Learning
Tammy Heflebower, Jan K. Hoegh, Philip B. Warrick, and Jeff Flygare
Designed specifically for K–12 teachers, this resource details a sequential approach for adopting and implementing standards-based learning. The authors provide practical advice, real-world examples, and answers to frequently asked questions designed to support you through this important transition.
BKL044

A School Leader's Guide to Standards-Based Grading
Tammy Heflebower, Jan K. Hoegh, and Phil Warrick
Assess and report student performance with standards-based grading rather than using traditional systems that incorporate nonacademic factors. Learn to assess and report performance based on prioritized standards, and gain effective strategies for offering students feedback on their progress.
BKL019

Connecting Through Leadership
Jasmine K. Kullar
The success of a school greatly depends on the ability of its leaders to communicate effectively. Rely on *Connecting Through Leadership* to help you strengthen your communication skills to inspire, motivate, and connect with every member of your school community.
BKF927

Messaging Matters
William D. Parker
Harness the power of messaging to create a culture of acknowledgment, respect, and celebration. Written specially for leaders, this title is divided into three parts, helping readers maximize their role as chief communicators with students, teachers, and parents and community.
BKF785

Solution Tree | Press   *a division of* Solution Tree

Visit SolutionTree.com or call 800.733.6786 to order.